One Ugandan's FAITH-FILLED Immigration Story

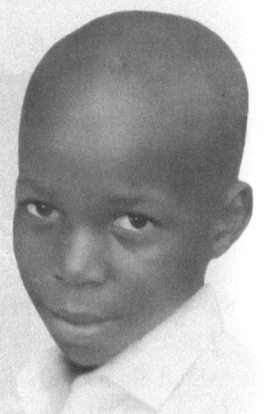

I Dreamed of SKYSCRAPERS

Derrick Kitayiga

LC record available at https://lccn.loc.gov/Library of Congress Cataloging-in-Publication Data
Names: Derrick Kitayiga
Title: I Dreamed of Skyscrapers: One Ugandan's Faith-Filled Immigration Story

Subjects: BIOGRAPHY & AUTOBIOGRAPHY / Cultural, Ethnic & Regional / African American & Black | YOUNG ADULT NONFICTION / Biography & Autobiography / Cultural, Ethnic & Regional | YOUNG ADULT NONFICTION / Social Topics / Emigration & Immigration

Description: Derrick Kitayiga woke up one morning from what he now sees as a God-sent dream. But a dream of moving from Kampala, Uganda, to the West is one thing; seeing it come to pass is quite another.

Identifiers: LCCN 2024903723 | paperback 9798990110809 | hardback 9798990110847 | e-book 9798990110816

To my beloved grandma, whose unwavering faith
and wisdom inspired every page within.
Your spirit lives on in me.

Author's Note

This memoir is a work of personal recollection and reflection. The events, dialogues, and experiences shared within these pages are based on the author's memory and perspective. While every effort has been made to portray accurate and authentic accounts, some details may have been altered or compressed for narrative purposes. Names, locations, and identifying characteristics of individuals may have been changed to protect their privacy. The intention of this memoir is to share personal growth, insights, and lessons learned, and it should not be interpreted as a definitive historical or factual account. The author acknowledges that memory can be subjective and that different individuals may recall events differently. This memoir is a sincere attempt to capture the essence of a life journey and is not intended to provide legal, medical, or professional advice. Readers are encouraged to approach these pages with an open heart, recognizing the unique nature of personal narratives and the complexity of human experiences.

Special Thanks

I could not have written this book without the help of some very special people.

Judah Dwight Sander, Nancy Bramlett, Susy Flory, Joyce Hightower, Lance Hahn, and Brian Kiley, thank you so much for all your help and encouragement.

Heavens Writers Group and BYA Writers group, your support has made all the difference.

Contents

Introduction

After I moved to California from Kampala, Uganda, in 2019, my new friends had all kinds of questions about my way of life because of the cultural diversity and ways of life that I introduced to the group. My answers only seemed to prompt more questions, so—even though I had been reluctant to pen my story, not wanting others to feel sorry for me—the inquiries made me think it would be easier just to write my story rather than repeat it over and over.

Before this book, I wrote short stories about other people, never my own because I didn't want to remind myself of the ups and downs I had been through. I finally thought it might be a good idea, though, and started trying to write everything down, but the more I wrote, the more I realized that I had not healed from most of the emotional scars. This got to me, and I stopped writing for a while to collect myself. It wasn't until I moved from Los Angeles to Sacramento, California, that the pastor of a young adult group I joined encouraged me to share my story so I could inspire and impact somebody else's life if they were going through a similar situation, When I told him I had wounds I didn't want to get back into, he suggested writing a memoir that didn't go deep emotionally but still told my story. After this possibility got into my head, I went back to writing and started thinking about which parts of my story I could write about, and this book is the result.

I hope my story provides
encouragement to those who are
facing immense challenges and
encountering discouragement from
various sources.

If you find yourself holding onto dreams that appear overwhelmingly grand, dreams that others may dismiss or discourage, I want to remind you of the significance of faith. Throughout the pages of this book, you will come to understand the central role faith has played in my own journey. It is through my unwavering trust in the Lord that I have found the strength and resilience to persevere in the face of adversity. I firmly believe in the greatness of His promises, for He never forgets them. So, as you begin reading this book, I urge you to keep pushing forward, keep holding onto your dreams, and keep placing your trust in the Lord. His faithfulness knows no bounds, and He has the power to guide you toward the fulfillment of your dreams.

Becoming

*O*nly an immigrant understands what it means to be one.

Why would an immigrant leave their motherland? I had the same question each time I saw people from different countries and cultures move to my homeland, but that was way before I moved far away myself. Just as every immigrant has their own reasons for why they move thousands of miles away from their homeland, I am no different.

I used to have a full name, just like any other person, but that was way before I was given the term "the immigrant." At first, I did not take that well. I would shut down that relationship quickly. I thought being called an immigrant was a way of being attacked, which was indeed the intention of some people who said it. However, the word immigrant has eventually become like music to my ears, because I hear it on the lips of friends. The word "immigrant" has led me to discover new friendships and connections that transcend cultural boundaries. It has opened doors to forge deep bonds with individuals from different backgrounds, creating a rich tapestry of shared experiences, stories, and perspectives. Through these friendships, I have gained a profound appreciation for the beauty of diversity and the strength that comes from learning about and embracing our differences.

Embracing my identity as an immigrant has helped me make friends because it has allowed me to authentically connect with others who have similar experiences. By proudly wearing the label of immigrant, I have found common ground with individuals who understand the trials, triumphs, and aspirations that come with building a new life in a foreign land. It has provided a foundation for meaningful conversations and mutual support.

How I Became an Immigrant

Uganda sits halfway around the world, deep in the east of the great African Continent. A British protectorate from 1894 until 1962, when it gained independence. Known as the "Pearl of Africa," Uganda is home to serene beauty consisting of tropical rainforests, crystal clear lakes, varied landscapes, and a snowcapped mountain (Rwenzori). Uganda is also home to one of the sources of the Nile River. But many in the West know my motherland more for its notorious dictator—Idi Amin. He is also known as the "Last King of Scotland," and his reign was marked by brutality, repression, and human rights abuses. My age has known only one president—Yoweri Kagutta

Museveni, who has been in power for almost four decades. The capital city of Uganda, Kampala, is the largest city of Uganda, and it borders Lake Victoria, Africa's largest lake. Kampala is well-known for its rolling hills, which reach an elevation of up to 4,000 feet.

Small Beginnings

In the beginning was the Word and the Word was with God and the Word was God. In the same way, at the end of 1998, I found favor in the Lord and was born alive and kicking to a beautiful couple.

My parents met while working on a small subsistence farm on the outskirts of Kampala. My dad took care of the cattle, and my mom was in the poultry department. It was modern-day love at first sight. My mom and dad were still figuring out life together after having their first son, David, when my mom conceived me. However, because my parents had not planned for, nor were they capable of caring for, a second child, this added to their struggles mentally and financially.

Instead of growing up with my parents, I was raised in my grandparents' staunch Catholic home. To make a long story short, my coming into this world ended up causing my parents to get separated. My brother and I were in the middle of that fight. When my grandmother on my father's side heard of it, she intervened, and we ended up staying with her. Grandmother Robinah welcomed me and my brother with love and took care of us. I never got to know my parents much during my childhood.

My grandmother was a treasure of love, wisdom, and warmth. With her gentle smile and nurturing nature, she embodied the essence of care and compassion. Her eyes, sparkling with years of experience, reflected a lifetime of stories and cherished memories. Wrinkles gracefully traced her face, each line representing the joys and sadness she had embraced throughout her journey. Her touch carried a comforting embrace, bringing solace to those in need. In her presence, one found a sense of security and unconditional love. The wisdom she imparted flowed like a gentle river, offering guidance and lessons learned from a lifetime of instruction. Whether through her comfort, delicious homemade treats, or the stories she shared, her presence brought a sense of connection and a glimpse into the past.

My grandmother taught me so many things. She was an educated lady, loving, caring, understanding, and a mother of four—three daughters and a son. Beautiful, funny, selfless, and very protective, she was a doctor by profession. Unfortunately, she became a widow at a young age, losing her husband in a time of war. After her loss, she was so traumatized that she did not even want to be a doctor anymore. She decided to change some things in her life and do what made her happy. This included doing what gave her more peace and rest. She decided to use the little money she was left with to start a small restaurant, where she could get some income for herself and her grandkids.

I thought she was my actual mom for a long time because she was with me throughout every battle I had as a kid. She wouldn't eat before I did or even sleep before checking on me. At times when I was sad, she would crack jokes to cheer me up. She often told me stories of the past and about the history of my culture, and talked about how to live a better life.

Home

My grandmother's enchanting, three-bedroom house sat on a piece of land close to two acres. It embraced the allure of the past with its design and craftsmanship. From the classic pitched roof and charming dormer windows to the welcoming front porch, it was surrounded by fruit trees for every season—including mangoes, papaya, guavas, mulberries, pomegranates, avocados, and jackfruit—and flowerbeds. She also built a vast compound with a small play area for her grandkids and engaged in poultry farming. She even built a small wooden house on her roof for doves, who could start cooing early, so you had to be a deep sleeper to stay in bed. She would joke about the doves being her alarm.

Some cousins and two aunties also lived in the house. I met Aunty Ruth and Grandma's youngest daughter of the four children, Aunty Ronda, who loved hanging out with me because she thought I was a bright kid. She told me I demonstrated quick learning abilities, exhibited curiosity and a thirst for knowledge, possessed exceptional memory skills, displayed advanced language capabilities, and showed a natural inclination toward grasping complex concepts.

Ronda possessed a captivating physical presence. With her radiant smile and expressive eyes, she exuded warmth and approachability. Her features were gracefully defined, from her softly curved face to her beautifully styled hair. There was an air of elegance about her, reflected in her poised posture and movements. Whether in her fashionable attire or simple yet tasteful choices, she carried herself with confidence and a touch of sophistication. Her warm embrace was comforting and her touch was gentle, conveying love and care. She embodied a unique blend of beauty, grace, and inherent charm that left a lasting impression. Ronda attended university and would soon graduate, but when at home, she enjoyed teaching me many things. She liked fashion, so she started dressing me up like a fashionista, which I enjoyed so much because I wanted to look good. She started homeschooling me and teaching me how to play board games, like monopoly, at a very young age. By the time I was ready for school, the elementary school I was taken to allowed me to skip some classes because I knew almost everything that they taught in them, thanks to my aunty.

My school was one of the most prominent private schools in the area, though it was a small school compared to the government schools. It was located on the district's outskirts and was well-known for its academic performance on a district level. Many parents wanted to get their kids to that school, but it had close to four hundred students and couldn't accept more due to its size—it was in a busy area surrounded by houses and businesses, which prevented it from being able to expand.

My elementary school was miles away from the comfort of home, in a different town, and I would walk to school every day, leaving just as the sun rose over the horizon. The path we traversed was more than just a stretch of dirt road; it was a passage adorned with picturesque landscapes—lush greenery that whispered stories of the wind, quaint farmhouses standing like sentinels of time, and the occasional clucking of chickens echoing through the air. Farmhouses, weathered by time, stood as silent witnesses to the changing seasons. My journey wasn't just about the distance covered but about the sensory symphony that accompanied me each day, and the kaleidoscope of sights and scents that made the journey as memorable as the destination itself. The dirt roads beneath my feet told tales of generations who had trodden the same path before me, imprinting the earth with the essence of community and shared history.

I was younger than my cousins and in a lower class than them, which meant I would leave school earlier than them. At first, I stayed at school, waited until their classes ended, and walked back home with them. This was until I made friends with my classmates who lived in the same area, and I started walking back home with some of them. Surprisingly, most of them were from the same hometown (Mpererwe), even though the school was in a different town.

A few months after I started school, Aunty Ronda left, and I never saw her again. I was told she had moved far away from home. However, I would talk to her on the phone sometimes, but I missed her so much because we had been so close. It took me a while to get used to not seeing her around.

I saw my father sometimes—when he came to visit my grandmother. On many occasions when he showed up, we never had any honest, love-filled father-and-son conversations. Remarkably, he only appeared whenever he learned of any wrongdoing on my part. Each encounter with my father meant an impending punishment, regardless of whether I was truly at fault. Throughout my childhood, I never witnessed a smile on my father's face; instead, an expression of anger always greeted me.

On one occasion, I found myself embroiled in a schoolyard altercation. A friend of mine had thrown a rock at a student from a higher grade, and while my friend fled the scene, I remained to face the consequences. The targeted student vented his frustration on me, attempting to initiate a fight. I defended myself admirably, but the situation escalated when he returned later with a group of friends, intent on a collective assault. Though I possessed self-defense skills, battling four individuals proved insurmountable. After enduring a thrashing, they eventually released me. In that moment, fueled by desperation, I seized a rock and hurled it, striking one of them on the back of the head, causing him to bleed. Realizing the danger, I fled the scene. Upon arriving home, I chose to keep the incident concealed, but within a few hours, the injured boy, accompanied by his enraged parents, arrived on our doorstep. My father, upon learning of the incident, never bothered to ask for an explanation—perhaps why I resorted to throwing the rock. I recall the murderous gaze in his eyes, followed by one of the most unforgettable beatings of my life.

This made me never want to see my father again because I was so scared of him, and my heart would race even when I saw someone who looked like him on the streets. It made me sad when I saw other kids having fun with their fathers, and I always wondered why my father did not like me.

Under my grandmother's care, I was this little peaceful, bright ambivert who loved music, soccer, and video games. And when I was around people I was used to, I was a very playful boy with lots of dreams. I kept adding to my list of dreams every time I learned something new and exciting.

My Young Faith

I became the only nondenominational Christian in the family at the age of five after accepting Christ as my

Savior during an open-air crusade. A nondenominational Christian is a person who identifies as a Christian but does not align themself with any specific denomination or formalized religious organization within Christianity. Instead of following the doctrines, traditions, and hierarchical structures associated with a particular denomination, nondenominational Christians prioritize a more independent and flexible approach to their faith. In my mother tongue, this is called *mulokole*.

The open-air crusade movement hosts outdoor evening church services in an area for a specified period. This is done to tell the good news, win souls, strengthen Christianity, and plant churches in a particular place. They play worship music, preach, and then show a movie about Christianity.

The journey of how I became a Christian is a question I still ponder, marveling at my boldness and courage that seemed to come out of nowhere. It all started one day when a crusade was being held near my house. The appealing sounds of loud worship music caught my attention immediately. Despite this, I chose to stay home and listen to the distant echoes of what was happening. But the following day, the pull grew stronger, and I felt an irresistible temptation to see for myself what was unfolding. By the third day of the crusade, I gathered the courage to approach my grandmother and ask if I could attend. She knew our neighbors' kids were going and without hesitation, she granted me permission. Filled with anticipation, I joined my friends.

As we arrived at the bustling venue, the sounds of praise and worship washed over me, resonating deep within my soul. The crusade was a vibrant gathering that brought the spirit of worship and faith to an expansive grass soccer field adjacent to a bustling road. As we approached, we were greeted by a picturesque scene—the field was bathed in golden sunlight, its lush green carpet stretching out under the vast expanse of the sky. Colorful banners and flags fluttered in the gentle breeze, adding a festive touch to the atmosphere. The crowd gathered at the event was diverse, a mosaic of individuals from all walks of life. They formed a picture of unity, their shared purpose palpable in the air. Smiling faces radiated with hope, their eyes reflecting a deep sense of faith and conviction. Some wore traditional attire while others donned casual clothing, representing the vibrant mix of cultures and backgrounds present. Amid the sea of people, one person caught my attention—an elderly man in a white coat, his weathered face etched with wisdom and grace. He stood near the front, like a pillar of strength and reverence. His eyes sparkled with kindness, and his hands gently clasped a well-worn Bible. It was evident that his presence held significance as the crowd gravitated toward him, seeking his guidance.

Throughout the event, this man's voice rose above the others with unwavering passion and sincerity. His words painted vivid pictures of hope and love, captivating the hearts of those listening. Each expression on his face mirrored the depth of his emotions, from gentle smiles to furrowed brows, conveying the profound impact of the messages he shared. His presence and wise and inspiring words left an indelible impression, reminding everyone of the power of faith and the capacity to touch lives through love and compassion.

The atmosphere was charged with devotion, and the preaching stirred something profound within me. When the time came for those willing to accept Christ to come forward for prayer, an indescribable force seemed to beckon me, urging me to step out in faith. However, the presence of my friends made me hesitate. I wrestled with the fear of embarrassment, desperately searching for someone familiar to lead the way. But to my dismay, none of my companions displayed the same inclination. My heart raced as if I stood on the precipice of a life-altering opportunity. The internal struggle became overwhelming, and I moved aimlessly, hoping to calm my racing heart. Time seemed to stretch on, the nearly five minutes feeling like an eternity.

The love of music and the fascinating story of a Savior drew me in with an irresistible force. There was no way I could let this Holy Spirit wave pass me by. The power of music lured me closer to the truth and the greatest gift of all — salvation. Finally, with a resolute decision, I started moving toward the front, casting aside my concerns about onlookers. I joined the throng of individuals eagerly seeking spiritual transformation and made my way forward, humble and expectant. I was asked if I was ready to embrace salvation, a question my heart answered with unwavering determination. In that moment, I knew I had taken a significant step toward a new chapter in my life, a step that would shape my faith and transform my perspective forever.

My Family's Reaction

However, I couldn't help but worry about my staunch Catholic grandmother's reaction to my decision. It took me some time to gather the courage to share the news with her. To my surprise, she showed little concern as long as I continued attending church every Sunday. Her acceptance eased my anxieties and allowed me to embrace my newfound faith more fully. Yet, within my immediate circle of family, I faced a different obstacle. I had three cousins and a brother who viewed my decision to become a born-again Christian with disdain. They saw it as an opportunity to exert peer pressure, assuming I would soon abandon my faith under their influence. They bombarded me with negative remarks, attempting to undermine my commitment. In their attempts to mock and belittle my faith, they even bestowed upon me the nickname "pastor." While I preferred to be called by my given name, their persistence in using this moniker proved unyielding. As the youngest among us, I found myself subject to their authority and control; that of the older cousins—Abraham, Isaac, and Jacob—and of my brother. Abraham, being seven years my senior, held the most sway over our collective decisions, though disagreements occasionally arose.

Despite my subordinate position in our familial hierarchy, I refused to be passive. I developed a rebellious streak, feeling overwhelmed by the constant stream of commands and expectations. Consequently, clashes and confrontations ensued, particularly when my brother and cousins attempted to impose their will upon me. I learned to stand up for my rights when they were violated, and to assert myself against those who sought to take advantage of me.

- 2 -

A Cohesive Team

Although our family dynamics often presented difficulties, our unity prevailed outside of the home. Socially, we were a cohesive team, always in agreement and relentless in pursuing our collective goals. We moved as a group, and anyone who dared to challenge one of us found themselves at odds with all of us. Consequently, our peers learned not to trifle with any member of our tight-knit group.

Our competitive spirit knew no bounds, and we became friendly rivals in every conceivable activity. From soccer to video games, volleyball to track, tumbling to academic pursuits, each day brought a new contest. Slacking off was not an option as it would be met with relentless teasing and encouragement until improvement was achieved. Trash talk became our chosen method of motivation, driving each other to reach our fullest potential. However, this spirited competition occasionally spilled over into encounters with other children, transforming winning into a matter of pride.

Being the youngest among my cousins and brother often made me the target of their jests. I was seen as the weak spot in the group, unable to defend myself adequately. Consequently, I became the one who sought assistance from the "big guns" whenever I faced something difficult. Despite this vulnerability, I managed to find solace in the one area where I excelled beyond my older counterparts—academics. When the school holidays arrived, I would eagerly inspect my report card, where I was encouraged by my academic achievements before celebrating our collective successes.

Throughout it all, the competitive spirit that defined our relationships created a constant source of headaches for our grandmother and aunt. They tried to shield us from engaging in risky behaviors, but our unyielding drive for excellence made it a daunting task.

Amid the ups and downs of family dynamics, I grew on my journey of faith, holding on to the love of music and the unwavering story of a Savior. It was a path that was hard at times, but it ultimately led me to discover a deeper connection with my spirituality and a profound sense of purpose.

Unfortunate Consequences

Our youthful adventures were not without their fair share of mishaps and injuries. Our exuberant soccer matches were sources of both joy and chaos. With each thunderous kick came the risk of shattered glass windows, much to the dismay of our neighbors. Complaints would often flood in as a testament to the sheer power behind our fervent strikes. The sound of shattering glass served as an unwelcome reminder of the collateral damage we left in our wake.

Despite the unfortunate consequences of our soccer games, we reveled in the pure joy of the sport. The ball became an extension of ourselves, our feet working in perfect harmony to navigate the field with skill and finesse. The intensity of the matches, fueled by our unyielding competitiveness, often resulted in unforeseen accidents and injuries.

Amid the cacophony of laughter and the thud of the ball against flesh, bones occasionally met their limits, bending and fracturing under the pressure of our athletic endeavors. Yet rather than seek immediate help, we chose to keep our injuries hidden, fearing the repercussions that would surely follow if our mischief was discovered. And then there were the instances when our curiosity got the best of us. A momentary lapse in judgment led to objects finding their way into the most unlikely places—ears and noses becoming temporary homes for small trinkets or foreign debris. In our youthful naivety, we believed that concealing our wounds and foreign objects would somehow make the situations more manageable.

In retrospect, our youthful recklessness held a certain charm. The scars we bore, both visible and hidden, became badges of honor, symbols of the spirited adventures that shaped our childhood. Though we unintentionally caused havoc and disruption, we held on to the joy of those carefree moments, cherishing the memories of soccer games that left their marks on our bodies and the shattered windows that served as a testament to our boundless energy.

Bunny Raising

One day, after persistently requesting for a while, our grandmother granted our wish and gave us bunnies to raise. We had been asking her for this for some time, and she finally decided to make it happen. However, before doing so, she took the time to thoroughly explain all the rules and regulations, ensuring that we understood and agreed to follow them before entrusting us with the bunnies. She made sure we were knowledgeable about their dietary preferences, the identifiable signs of illness, how to clean their habitat, and how to feed them. By the end of her explanations, we felt confident we had the knowledge we needed to care for these adorable creatures. As an additional thoughtful gesture, our grandmother even hired a carpenter to construct a hutch for the bunnies. Once the hutch was completed, we excitedly placed some female and one male bunny inside, marking the beginning of our journey as bunny raisers.

Every day in the morning and evening, we would go out in search of the Macdonald weed, which was the bunnies' favorite of everything we fed them. However, at times we couldn't find enough, so we'd approach our friends, kindly requesting access to their gardens. Fortunately, many of them willingly granted us permission, as they wanted to rid their own gardens of these unwanted plants.

After a while, one of the bunnies surprised us with her pregnancy. Initially, we didn't realize what was happening. The bunny seemed slower than usual, and her belly had noticeably expanded, raising concerns among us about her health. Seeking guidance, we turned to our wise grandmother, hoping she could shed some light on the situation. As soon as she examined the bunny, her face lit up with a knowing smile, and she joyfully announced that we were soon to become parents to a litter of baby bunnies. At first, her words puzzled us, and we exchanged confused glances. Sensing our bewilderment, our grandmother couldn't help but chuckle, and then she explained that the bunny was pregnant. This revelation filled us with excitement, as it would be our first encounter with adorable baby bunnies. With eagerness, we started celebrating and making preparations under our grandmother's guidance, including gathering a cozy basket and lining it with soft, warm blankets to ensure the little ones would stay snug and comfortable. One early morning, the tranquility was abruptly shattered when one of my cousins let out a piercing scream while checking on the bunnies. In an instant, we all raced to the hutch, anxiety coursing through our veins. To our surprise, my cousin was clutching a hefty stick in his hand. Curiosity piqued, we questioned him about the commotion, and he informed us that there were tiny rats in the hutch.

Fearing for the safety of our pregnant bunny, our minds conjured up images of a menacing rodent that could harm her. With resolve etched on our faces, we armed ourselves with sticks too, poised to defend against any rat that dared to intrude. We meticulously scoured every nook and cranny of the hutch, but to our astonishment, no rats were found—only these miniature creatures with a rat-like appearance.

Perplexed by their presence, we collected the little ones, unsure of how to handle them. We feared the return of their mother, who might pose a threat to our beloved bunnies or join in a skirmish. Again, we turned to our wise and ever-reliable grandmother, beseeching her advice on what to do with these rat-like beings. As soon as she heard the news of rats in the bunnies' hutch, a hint of concern clouded her features, propelling her to investigate the situation firsthand. Upon reaching the cage, we still clutched our sticks, awaiting her verdict. However, when our grandmother's eyes fell upon the creatures, uncontrollable laughter erupted from her lips, after which she labeled us as "bad parents." Confusion knotted our brows as we struggled to comprehend her jest. It wasn't until she revealed the truth that our bewilderment gave way to sheer joy—the so-called rats were, in fact, the long-awaited young bunnies we had all been eagerly anticipating.

We couldn't believe it because they did not look like bunnies. They did not have hair on their bodies, and they were making weird, rat-like sounds. When she explained everything about bunnies, we pulled out our blanketed basket and covered all of them. Our grandmother taught us how to feed them and protect them adequately in the basket.

Daily Routines

My grandmother was very strict regarding bedtime, chores, and school. She had set a bedtime for us before midnight and a time for us to take naps during the day after lunch; although we could escape the house without her noticing and play soccer with friends, then come back later, and she never even saw.

She set chores for us: doing the dishes, cleaning the compound, and fetching water. Since we had no running water at the house, she gave us money so we could buy water, which some nearby places sold. We would fill our jerrycans and then carry them back home. It was not a hard job, though sometimes there were shortages, and we had to go to wells or boreholes to get water. These were up to two miles away and usually crowded because they were free. We had to wait in line for about an hour so we could fill up our jerrycans, but these were places where people would try anything. Those who never wanted to follow the rules or wait in line would just jump the line and fight anyone next in line to fill their jerrycan. These wells were places where no one wanted to be, but still, we needed the water, so we had to withstand every situation together.

Doing the dishes was the easiest chore for me, and I wouldn't mind doing that instead of fetching water or cleaning the compound. We had a big yard, which made cleaning the compound not an easy job—we had to use brooms to sweep the hundreds of tree leaves away every day.

Academics

My grandmother wanted me to be a doctor, and she was always reminding me of that. She was always proud to use my school report cards as an example to my cousins about performing well at school. Some of my cousins weren't as happy about my grades because theirs were bad, and at the end of each term, they'd hope I did badly so they would not get lectures from my grandmother. I could not help them with that because I enjoyed performing well.

Since there was no man in her house, my grandmother was very soft on us. We knew when she was really serious, but we also knew she was not going to punish us. We sometimes disobeyed, and she reached the point of realizing that we were getting spoiled if she did not do anything at all, so she ended up calling our uncle or my dad in case she needed any or all of us to be punished and put back in line.

I never missed my parents at all as a kid, and this was because of the selfless love of my grandmother Robinah. I could not have asked God for anyone better.

Insight

My immigration journey started with a dream. I didn't have school over the weekends, so one Saturday I spent most of the day playing soccer with my friends. By evening we were all sweaty and tired and wanted to go home, hydrate, eat, and rest.

I got home starving and couldn't wait to have some food. However, my grandmother had other priorities. She took one look at me and pointed to the bathroom.

"Go clean up."

"I'm hungry. What's there to eat?"

"Nothing until you shower and put on clean clothes."

"Come on," I wheedled. "I'm too hungry to move."

"Fine, but don't get in my kitchen until you look and smell better."

She went back to her baking. I growled at her. Behind her back, I gave her the dirtiest look I could conjure up. I should have saved my energy. I never won with my grandmother. Finally, I stomped off to shower. After I changed into the clean clothes my grandmother had set out for me, I sat down to a plate of chicken and rice—my favorite food. I ate like a starving man, barely tasting the food. With a satisfied sigh, I went to lie on my bed, my full belly lulling me into a deep sleep. The next thing I remember was being in the middle of a large, beautiful, and busy town with many skyscrapers. I admired all the new sights in this town as I made my way through the streets. I started walking toward the skyscrapers, and before I got there, I saw a couple of kids my age playing in a water fountain. I walked toward them and tried to ask for permission to join them, but none of those kids seemed to hear what I was saying. I raised my voice so I could get their attention. At the top of my lungs, I shouted, "Hey, do you think I can join you guys?" I realized I was dreaming when my loud yelling woke me up!

My grandmother padded into my room, leaned over me, and asked, "Are you okay?"

Confused, I sat up, realized it was the middle of the night, and fell back onto my pillow.

Grandmother kissed my forehead. "It was just a dream. Go back to sleep."

I closed my eyes, but sleep eluded me. I could visualize the city as though I had actually been there. I wanted to return to this beautiful place, so I tried to force myself to sleep so I could dream again, but I failed. I was woken up in the morning by doves cooing on the roof.

I did not share my dream with anyone because I did not want to look stupid. I had never seen a place with so many skyscrapers before, and I wished I could be in a place like that.

Mr. Zimbe

I liked most of my teachers; however, one of them stood out—Mr. Zimbe, my social studies teacher. From the moment I first laid eyes on him, I felt a sense of both awe and intimidation. Mr. Zimbe was larger than life, both physically and in his commanding presence. Standing tall at over six feet, his towering frame seemed to dominate the room. His broad shoulders and muscular build exuded strength and power, while his confident demeanor captured the attention of everyone around him.

Entering Mr. Zimbe's classroom was always an experience. The class only had a few students, which created an intimate atmosphere. Despite the missing windowpanes that let in the outside noise, the room was often filled with laughter and chatter, generating a joyful ambiance. The sunlight would filter through the broken windows, casting warm rays and creating playful shadows on the walls, which were adorned with colorful posters and student artwork. But as each class with Mr. Zimbe unfolded, suspense and anxiety would build within me. Known as a talkative and stubborn student, I often found myself in trouble for not containing my energy. However, things changed when I became the top performer in his class.

One particular day, after we took a test, Mr. Zimbe began handing out the results one by one, starting from the lowest performers. I anxiously awaited my turn, hoping that my hard work had paid off. But as he reached the end of the pile, my name had still not been called. Confusion and nervousness took hold of me, and I couldn't fathom what had happened to my answer sheet. Finally, when Mr. Zimbe read out the name of the second-best performer, it wasn't me, and my anxiety intensified. My mind raced with thoughts of lost papers and missed opportunities. Then, in an unexpected twist, he called out my name as the top performer. Disbelief filled his eyes as he handed me my test results.

From that moment on, Mr. Zimbe and I grew closer. He became not only my teacher but also a mentor and father figure. He went above and beyond to help me with my studies, ensuring I attended class and guiding me through challenging subjects. His care extended beyond the classroom; he even called my home when I didn't show up to school to make sure I was okay. I once mustered the courage to ask him why he chose to help me. He responded with a smile, telling me that he had never encountered a student who possessed both stubbornness and playfulness while consistently performing well in his class. That revelation solidified our bond, and his dedication to my education became a constant source of inspiration for which I will always be grateful.

The Overseas

One day, as I walked home with my friends, we began a lively conversation about school, our activities at home, and even our shared passion for video games. Amid our discussions, I overheard my friends discussing something called "the overseas." Intrigued, I couldn't help but express my initial skepticism. Being someone who grew up in a trash-talking environment, I had developed a tendency to be quick-witted and dismissive about topics that seemed unfamiliar or far-fetched. So, without giving it much thought and believing this to be yet another of their elaborate stories that blurred the line between reality and fiction, I began to trash-talk their conversation. I overwhelmed them with my banter, unintentionally derailing the discussion and preventing them from elaborating further. I thought their tall tale didn't warrant serious consideration. We switched to different conversations, but little did I know I would soon be proven wrong when I heard the same story from a credible source—a movie. I was not a fan of movies, but my cousins were watching one, and since I was younger and wanted to be around them, I had no choice but to watch with them.

This movie was called *007 Die Another Day*, and I saw some overseas cities with their many skyscrapers. I couldn't believe my eyes and remembered the dream I'd had of a big, beautiful city with many skyscrapers. I was surprised and very curious, but my pride made me not want to go back to my friends to get the rest of the story about overseas countries I had trash-talked.

You Can't Google That

Growing up in a third-world country, access to technology and the internet was a luxury that many of us couldn't afford, so researching on Google was impossible. The limitations I faced made me rely on alternative methods of finding information. Libraries were a treasure trove for me. I would spend countless hours flipping through books, encyclopedias, and magazines, hoping to stumble upon the answers to my questions. The smell of old books and the sound of turning pages became my companions on my quest for knowledge. But even our libraries had their limitations. Many of them lacked updated resources, especially on current events or the latest technological advancements. The books were often outdated, and finding specific information required patience, perseverance, and sometimes sheer luck.

Beyond libraries, I relied on human resources to expand my understanding of the world. Conversations with friends, neighbors, and elders in the community became invaluable. Sharing stories, experiences, and personal anecdotes became a way to piece together the bigger picture of what lay beyond my country. These interactions not only provided me with information but also fostered a sense of community and connection that would shape my worldview.

DIY Learning

Furthermore, growing up in a third-world country meant embracing a DIY (do-it-yourself) mentality. We had to become resourceful and innovative to solve problems and find answers. Experimentation and hands-on learning became the norm. Whether it was fixing broken appliances, constructing makeshift tools, or discovering alternative solutions, we learned to adapt and make the most of the limited resources available to us.

I was always acutely aware of the socioeconomic disparities and systemic issues that plagued our society. Witnessing poverty, inequality, and a lack of access to basic necessities on a daily basis left a lasting impact on me. It fueled my long-term plan to learn and find ways to contribute positively to my community and seek solutions to this lack of resources.

Looking back, the absence of instant information at my fingertips taught me the value of patience, resourcefulness, and human connections. It instilled in me a deep appreciation for the power of education and the importance of thorough research. While the world has since become more connected and information is more accessible, I carry with me the resilience, creativity, and adaptability that emerged from those circumstances. And I knew I could find out more about big cities in other countries this way.

In my relentless pursuit of knowledge, I devised creative methods to extract information from my friends, so, while on our way home after our classes, I'd seize the opportune moment and casually reintroduce the topic, playfully bantering and jesting that they knew nothing about it, as I had cunningly planned. Initially, my friends were uninterested in rehashing the conversation about what life was like overseas, but my subtle bait gradually piqued their curiosity. Eventually, they grew tired of my teasing that they knew nothing and their anger fueled them to prove me wrong. They embarked on a quest for references and evidence, passionately sharing their findings with me. Overwhelmed with excitement, I hung on to their every word, longing for each discourse to continue uninterrupted. The wealth of information gleaned from these exchanges lingered in my thoughts, resonating deeply wherever I sought solitude. The concept of countries over the sea fascinated me, given my origins in Uganda's landlocked position in East Africa, far removed from any oceans or seas. Though I had never beheld the sea firsthand, I grasped its essence through my understanding of the word. Nevertheless, comprehending the notion of "overseas" proved elusive.

The plethora of information I received surpassed my capacity to process and believe it, thus sowing doubt about the validity of such wonders. The outside world seemed surreal, mind-boggling, almost too marvelous to be real. Yet, the thought continued to tantalize my imagination, even as I questioned the authenticity of the stories relayed to me. Watching *007*

No Time to Die repeatedly fueling my fascination with its thrilling adventures and extraordinary accounts that stretched beyond believability, much like the experiences shared by the people I met.

- 4 -

The Magazine and Connection

fter a prolonged period of setting aside my pursuit of the overseas, one of my friends approached me with utmost conviction regarding the wonders of the outside world. He sought me out at my residence, driven by his relentless desire to prove a point. Our conversations were often lengthy and spirited, as we engaged in a constant battle of asserting our correctness.

Accompanying him was a peculiar book, which immediately piqued my interest. He expressed his intention to show me something within its pages, prompting us to find a comfortable spot to explore its contents. The book was a tome unlike any other I had encountered before. Calling it *the magazine*, it held an air of mystery, leaving me perplexed as to its significance. This book was a visual marvel, featuring an array of breathtaking photographs that displayed the outside world, complete with names of countries and islands. The sheer incredibility of it all overwhelmed me. Even familiar places from movies and towering skyscrapers, which perfectly echoed my cherished dreams, had their place within those pages.

I found myself repeatedly flipping through the book, captivated by the profound beauty it contained. My friend's question, "Do you believe me now?" echoed in the air. Though I typically resisted conceding defeat in our arguments, this time I had no ground to stand on. I could only silently observe, absorb, and learn. My friend's point had been convincingly made.

As I immersed myself in the book's mesmerizing imagery, my eyes widened at the uncontainable wonder. Those enchanting locations rekindled the excitement I'd felt upon first hearing about the outside world. I delved into its pages again and again, until the desire to experience it all firsthand became insatiable. Eventually, I found the courage to approach my friend and ask to borrow his book for a day, as if I had never explored its contents before. Though I'd flipped through it several times, the urge to delve deeper and uncover every hidden treasure within this book's pages was irresistible. The more time my friend allowed me to spend with his magazine, the more it would cement his victory, so he graciously allowed me to borrow it for a single night, with plans to retrieve it the following day.

Just One Day

On that particular day, everyone in my household became increasingly curious about my secluded behavior, as I remained locked away in my room most of the time. Concerned, my grandmother even speculated that I might be unwell, but that was far from the truth. As night fell, my eyes widened in awe yet again at each page's breathtaking wonders. A burning desire ignited within me, yearning to witness these remarkable places firsthand. I made a solemn promise to myself that one day I would set foot in one of those extraordinary locations and bask in its unparalleled beauty. Even at that tender age, embarking on an overseas journey became a cherished dream for me to pursue.

The following morning, in the early hours, I eagerly shared the magazine with my cousins. As they perused its contents, I passionately declared my intent to visit one of those enchanting destinations someday. To my delight, my cousins shared the same fervor as me, for they, too, were fascinated by the allure of exploration. As the saying goes, birds of a feather flock together. However, my cousins soon began deriding the idea, mocking my aspirations, until their words ignited a blazing anger within me. Fuming, I snatched the magazine from their hands and stormed off, consumed by thoughts of proving them wrong.

Returning home, I distanced myself from my cousins, eagerly anticipating my friend's arrival to retrieve his cherished book. When he finally appeared to take it back, I couldn't help but inquire about its origin. He disclosed that the book belonged to his uncle, who resided overseas. His uncle had returned for a visit, a revelation that seemed surreal but was sweet music to my ears. The excitement surged within me as the realization dawned that my dream of exploring distant lands might not be as far-fetched as I'd once believed. I wondered if I might meet a man who had experienced being overseas firsthand. Although uncertain if he had visited all the places mentioned in the book, I eagerly hoped he could enlighten me with further details about those remarkable locations.

I approached my friend again, requesting the privilege of meeting his uncle to talk about the wonders of other lands across the seas. He seemed hesitant, due to his uncle's busy schedule, but he promised to inquire on my behalf. The two days that followed felt interminable, akin to a week passing by. Regrettably, the answer my friend returned with was not the one I had fervently prayed for. His uncle was not prepared to indulge in such a discussion with a young individual like me. This news shattered my heart, as I had believed I was on the brink of accessing invaluable firsthand information. Nevertheless, I found solace and gratitude in knowing that my friend had made an earnest effort on my behalf.

With unwavering faith, my longing to know more felt like a divine calling, instilled by God with a purpose in mind. Despite my disappointment, my trust in the journey remained steadfast. Each encounter, whether fruitful or seemingly fruitless, became part of the tapestry guiding me toward a deeper understanding of myself and the world. I embraced patience and perseverance, knowing that God's timing was perfect. With this faith as my guiding light, I was determined to keep exploring the wonders of life overseas, knowing that the right opportunities and revelations would unfold when the time was right.

Persistence

I tenaciously persisted in my quest, seeking out individuals who possessed greater insights beyond what I already knew. After many years of seeking, my path intersected with an intriguing individual, John, a seasoned older veteran who had retired from his noble service. It was evident that his life had been one of dedication to duty and sacrifice. His rugged and weathered appearance told the story of having spent countless years braving the elements and traversing treacherous terrains. Despite the challenges he had endured, John's strong and toned build reflected the discipline and grit that defined his service years. Traces of battles fought, both physical and emotional, were etched upon his skin in the form of scars and injuries, each marking a moment of bravery and resilience. Yet, amid the signs of his struggles, there was an air of wisdom and authority exuded by his gray hair and beard, giving him a distinguished air. John stood tall, carrying the pride of his service in every step he took. His life as a veteran was etched in his very being, a testament to his unwavering commitment and sacrifice for a cause greater than himself.

The setting of our encounter added to its interesting nature—a soccer field. Though my regular attendance at this field was due to my team's engagements, on this occasion, I had ventured to observe other teams in action. Unbeknownst to me, destiny had arranged for both John and me to be spectators, ardently supporting the same team. Little did I expect the extraordinary turn of events that unfolded when I heard him casually liken one of the players to a "French striker." The impact of those words reverberated within me, awakening a dormant memory of an article in the magazine that bore the word "French."

From that instant, my interest swiftly shifted from the ongoing soccer game to the wealth of knowledge this older gentleman possessed about the French. I approached him, introducing myself and divulging my own soccer-playing background—which piqued his curiosity. In turn, he shared fragments of his life story. I began bombarding him with an array of questions about the French. He was thrilled to answer, and he genuinely enjoyed sharing his stories. He admitted that he didn't know much about the French, apart from their soccer team, but he was knowledgeable about the British.

The British

Although I wasn't particularly interested in that topic, I didn't want to turn down the kind gentleman, so I also encouraged him to tell me about "the British"—a term I wasn't familiar with. I listened, but my attention wavered. It was only when he mentioned that it was an overseas territory that I suddenly snapped out of my daze. Perplexed, I double-checked to ensure I had heard correctly. "Did you say Britain is an overseas territory?" To my surprise, he confirmed it. I couldn't help but wonder how he had acquired such knowledge about Britain. My suspicions of him fabricating stories began to arise, but then I discovered that he had a daughter residing there.

I was eager to understand how his daughter ended up in England and the story behind her journey, and whether he had ever visited England himself. In response, he shared that his daughter had obtained a scholarship to study in England, but he had never personally been there. Nonetheless, they stayed connected through phone calls and the internet, allowing his daughter to share her experiences and updates with him.

When he mentioned the internet, I realized it was a concept I wasn't well-versed in. Intrigued, I sought clarification from him, asking how he got internet on his phone, and he graciously pulled out his smart phone so he could explain its workings. "Imagine the internet as a vast network of interconnected highways, allowing information to travel from one place to another," he said. "When you use your phone or any other device to connect to the internet, you're essentially joining this massive network of interconnected devices."

John was the only person who had taken the time to address all my questions, skillfully guiding me through unfamiliar territory. I appreciated his patience and ability to provide clear explanations. Armed with all the new information, my mind filled with vivid images of England, and I couldn't help but yearn to experience it firsthand and access the wonders of the internet. I expressed my gratitude to him for generously sharing his time and knowledge.

On my journey home, thoughts of our conversation lingered in my mind. The wealth of information I had received was overwhelming, and I struggled to process it all. Days passed, yet my imagination continued to run wild, conjuring up images of England that seemed almost too enchanting to be real. Nevertheless, I held unwavering trust in the words of the older man, never doubting the authenticity of his accounts. This only fueled my desire to delve further into the possibilities that lay beyond my current circumstances. I couldn't help but believe there was a higher purpose to our meeting beyond the surface level of discussing soccer and overseas territories. The way he effortlessly shared his knowledge felt like a guiding hand directing me toward a path I had not yet fully explored.

This encounter reaffirmed my belief in the power of unexpected connections and the potential for divine intervention on my journey of seeking answers. It reminded me that sometimes, when we are open and receptive, the right people come into our lives at precisely the right moment to offer guidance and inspiration.

Scholarships

Upon arriving home, I headed straight to my room, seeking solace to process the multitude of questions swirling in my mind about the prospect of scholarships to foreign lands. I regretted not inquiring more about the specifics of John's daughter's scholarship. However, the confines of my room proved too stifling for the curiosity that consumed me. Unable to contain my inquiries any longer, I ventured out to seek answers from anyone available in the household.

To my disappointment, the only individuals present were my cousins, who were engrossed in a video game. "Hey, guys, do you know anything about scholarships or applying for financial aid for college?"

One of my cousins, still immersed in the game, looked up with a halfhearted smile and said, "Uh, not really. Scholarships can be pretty confusing, you know? We haven't really looked into it ourselves."

The other cousin chimed in, "Yeah, it's a whole big thing. You might want to talk to someone more knowledgeable about that stuff, like school counselors."

I felt a bit disheartened by their casual dismissal of my questions, but I reminded myself that finding solutions required persistence. I knew each encounter with information was a piece of a puzzle being laid out before me, shaping me and preparing me for what lay ahead. No effort toward seeking knowledge was wasted, and in due time, the right doors would open and the right opportunities would present themselves. In the quiet moments of contemplation, I often found myself expressing gratitude to a higher power for these encounters. I embraced the uncertainties of the future with optimism, knowing that I was not alone in my journey and that divine guidance was ever present.

Christmas

*I*n the year 2004, when late November rolled around, excitement of the upcoming Christmas holidays began to build. Christmas holds a special place in my heart, as it encompasses everything I adore—vibrant decorations adorning our home, enchanting tales of Jesus Christ, delectable feasts, and the cherished reunion of my extended family, some of whom lived far away. Despite being surrounded by a family that did not embrace faith in Christ, Christmas was still observed as a tradition. Unlike others who focused on gift-giving, our family festivities revolved around a profound sense of togetherness. We embraced one another, cherishing the love that bound us as a family. However, the true significance of the holiday and the essence of Jesus were often overlooked. In search of a deeper understanding of my childhood experience of receiving Jesus, I took it upon myself to attend a Christmas morning church service each year, where I could genuinely learn about and connect with the teachings of Jesus.

Being in the company of my relatives was a source of immense joy for me, as our family was known for its abundance of laughter and humorous exchanges. There was never a dull moment during this festive season, and the air was filled with mirth and amusement. Together, we enjoyed activities such as watching movies, hiking, bicycling, and playing board games—which often brought out my competitive nature.

Moreover, my grandmother seemed to transform her house into a culinary paradise during this time. Food, another highlight of the season, brought immense joy to my heart. The aroma of delicious foods continually wafted through the air, including that of my absolute favorite—the mouthwatering combination of matooke, rice, and succulent meat. Made from starchy green bananas that were skillfully peeled, steamed, and expertly mashed into a delectable meal, it never failed to satisfy the taste buds. To complement its rich flavors, it was often served alongside tender meat or flavorful beans, making it a deeply satisfying and cherished part of our holiday feasts. As a child, I savored every bite, relishing the flavors as if it were my last meal.

I also found great delight in knowing that I wouldn't be left alone to tackle the mountain of dishes after every meal because my only job was to do the dishes, but there were always willing hands ready to help. My grandparents' house served as the hub for our extensive family, so the holiday season was characterized by a constant stream of new faces, and I had the pleasure of meeting new relatives each Christmas. The season truly embodied a sense of togetherness, warmth, and celebration, leaving indelible memories etched in my heart year after year.

Sharing Our Stories

During this cherished period, our nightly routine involved congregating in the living room after dinner, where we would watch movies or engage in heartfelt discussions about life and how each person navigated their obstacles. On one particular evening, no one was in the mood for a movie, and I seized the opportunity. With enthusiasm, I asked if I could share something intriguing I had learned about "the overseas." Eager to highlight the breadth of information I had amassed, I began to passionately relay the details and recount the source of my newfound wisdom. I described encountering a magazine for the first time in my life and the invaluable insights shared by the elderly gentleman whose daughter resided in England.

However, to my astonishment, the most unexpected turn of events occurred when the family conversation shifted to discussions about the outside world. I soon realized that I needed to humble myself and assume a listening role, as it became apparent that my family possessed a wealth of knowledge that surpassed my initial assumptions. Their narratives and experiences depicted a familiarity with the outside world that extended far beyond my own limited exposure, leaving me in awe of their insights.

In the following days, I pondered the fragments of information that had been shared with me. One striking revelation was that some members of our own family resided in England, a fact I had been oblivious to until that moment. The realization was a profound surprise. Questions swirled in my mind about this unseen part of our family—did they know about me? Had they ever returned to our homeland? How did they end up in England? I yearned to uncover the missing pieces of this familial puzzle. I bombarded my relatives with an array of inquiries, but my enthusiasm soon began to overshadow their patience, and my attempts to redirect the focus back to my burning questions proved fruitless. Undeterred, I resolved to remain vigilant about listening to family news in case our family members from England paid us a visit, so I could meet them, learn about their experiences, and satiate my curiosity about life there.

In the midst of this waiting period, I made promises to myself and prayed fervently to God, seeking guidance on how I could one day fulfill my dream of exploring the outside world. Thoughts of the unknown intrigued me wherever I went—did people who lived overseas have schools and hospitals, did they speak the same language, did they have presidents, and what kind of food did they enjoy? I found myself engrossed in the subject of history. Learning about people from the outside world who had ventured into my country, and the complex history of colonization, intrigued me immensely.

My cousins often teased and dismissed my dreams, insisting that such aspirations were merely figments of my imagination that were unattainable and bound to remain unfulfilled. Their constant stream of negative comments attempted to dampen my spirit, including citing the high costs and the need for influential connections to embark on such a journey. While their observations held some truth, they failed to extinguish the flame of hope within me. I held steadfast in my faith, trusting that God would guide me on this path.

My Grandmother

Christmas passed and school resumed. With my cousins and brother now attending a boarding school, I was the sole student at home. The days became monotonous, save for the occasional video game session that offered temporary distraction. During those times, my grandmother and Aunt Ruth, who was also my grandmother's daughter, were my sole companions. One night, while I was engrossed in playing video games in my room, my grandmother went out with friends. Late in the night, I heard her return, but I decided not to disturb her. The next morning, my auntie rather than my grandmother woke me up from my deep slumber. Still groggy, I sensed an air of nervousness in her voice as she hurriedly urged me to get ready for school. At first, I paid little attention, attributing her demeanor to the early hour. But as my senses gradually awakened, I couldn't help but wonder why my auntie appeared so apprehensive. Upon completing my preparations, I made my way to the living room, eager to start the day. However, my auntie prevented me from entering, instead delivering my breakfast to my room with tear-filled eyes. She instructed me to head straight to school and started making numerous phone calls, ensuring I remained unaware of the conversations taking place.

Confused and unsettled, I left the house and embarked on my journey to school. Throughout the day, a sense of unease enveloped me, rendering it difficult to focus on my studies. Concerned classmates inquired about my well-being, but I couldn't articulate the underlying turmoil plaguing my mind. Deep within, I sensed something was amiss. As soon as the school day concluded, my eagerness to return home and uncover the truth intensified. Arriving at the house, the sight that greeted me shattered my hopes— ambulance lights flashing and my grandmother being tenderly placed on a medical stretcher. An oxygen mask covered her face and she looked bewildered. I was filled with confusion as I stepped into the house, desperately seeking my aunt's presence to shed light on why my grandma was being rushed to the hospital in an ambulance. Tears streamed down my aunt's face as I approached her, my heart pounding with anxiety. When I inquired about the situation, she revealed that my grandmother had lost consciousness and required immediate medical attention.

In the past, whenever my grandmother fell ill, she would either visit the hospital with me or venture there alone, so I couldn't fathom why an ambulance had been summoned this time. I implored my aunt to let me accompany them to the hospital. Yet, she insisted I wait until she was ready to accompany me. Throughout the evening, relatives and friends arrived at our home, offering support and solace. Their conversations with my aunt inadvertently revealed the name of the hospital where my grandmother had been taken—an unfamiliar name to my ears.

The following day, it wasn't possible to visit her and still make it to school, but my aunt informed me that we would visit her during lunchtime. We hailed a taxi and rode to the hospital, which turned out to be an awe-inspiring structure. Its vastness overwhelmed me, as I had never before encountered such an expansive medical facility. Armed with the room number and directions, we eventually reached the intensive care unit (ICU), where my grandmother was located. Regrettably, I was unable to approach her bedside; I could only catch a glimpse through a small window. Yearning to connect with her, I called out to my grandmother, assuming she was merely asleep. but it seemed as though my voice couldn't reach her. Troubled by her unresponsiveness, I turned to my aunt for answers. However, she was too engrossed in her tears to offer a reply. Uncertain of how to proceed, I returned to the window and watched my grandmother slumbering, feeling a sense of helplessness envelop me. Before leaving, I questioned when my grandmother would wake up and return home. Although I received no definite answer, I was advised to pray fervently for her recovery.

On our way back home, I persisted in my inquiries about what had caused my grandmother's prolonged slumber. My aunt initially hesitated to disclose the details but eventually revealed that my grandmother had suffered a fall during the night, presumably resulting in a stroke. The distressing part was that no one discovered her until early morning, hours after she had fallen, lying unconscious and vulnerable on the cold floor. It was nothing short of a miracle that she still drew breath when my aunt awoke. Terrified upon finding her and unable to detect any pulse, she feared the worst, but she called a doctor, who examined my grandmother and determined that she was still breathing.

After a week and several days, my grandmother regained consciousness and was able to breathe once again without the aid of machines. However, she had lost feeling and mobility in her left leg. Despite undergoing scans that revealed no fractures or major injuries, she was informed that the stroke was the cause. Strangely, my grandmother had no recollection of the events of that fateful night.

When my grandmother returned home, I witnessed a change in her demeanor. A woman of immense strength, she had always concealed her pain, but for the first time, I glimpsed her vulnerability. She yearned to regain her mobility but found herself confined to a wheelchair, gradually accepting the reality that she would always require assistance to move. My grandmother's body was forever altered. The stroke, like a relentless cancer, consumed her, starting with her leg and eventually spreading throughout. In time, she reached a point when each limb lay motionless, her existence defined by lying on her back. Throughout this painful ordeal, I fervently prayed, beseeching God for a miracle. I sought the support of every prayer warrior I knew, hoping for divine intervention. Yet, the long-awaited miracle failed to materialize.

Avoiding her room became a common practice for me as witnessing her in such a state was unbearable. Peering through her window became my way of checking on her, but I couldn't fathom the depth of agony she experienced—a pain I wished never to comprehend.

– 6 –

Other Family

Months flew by, and a glimmer of hope in the form of long-awaited good news finally graced my life. My distant relatives hailing from England were planning to visit us during the forthcoming Christmas season. The mere thought of their arrival filled me with boundless excitement.

Whispers of preparations echoed through the air, along with discussions centered around the arrangements for their warm welcome at the airport. The anticipation consumed me, and I couldn't contain my eagerness. I mustered the courage to ask if I could be one of the fortunate few chosen to greet them at the airport. Considering my tender age, I was still unfamiliar with the whereabouts of such a significant place. Despite the organizers' initial reluctance to include me, they quickly realized that declining my request would only lead to a barrage of questions demanding an explanation. Thus, they had no choice but to concede.

Their schedule revealed that their flight would arrive well past midnight—way beyond my usual bedtime—yet, when the time to depart approached, I displayed no signs of drowsiness, much to their surprise. In truth, this was a deliberate act on my part to avoid being left behind. Although my body longed for rest, I didn't want anyone to know. It took nearly twenty minutes of the hour-long drive in a van for slumber to claim me. I struggled against fatigue, but my efforts proved futile, and by the time I awoke, I found myself tucked back in bed. Confusion gripped me, and I pondered what had transpired. I recalled boarding the van, yet the memory of arriving at the airport eluded me. The darkness in the room indicated it was still nighttime, and everyone lay sound asleep. Initially, I questioned whether I was trapped in a dream, only to realize it was all too real. Fear of the dark prevented me from venturing out of bed, so I remained there until sleep overcame me once more.

The enchanting melodies of nightingales woke me in the early morning. Unable to return to sleep, I noticed the sun's ascent and remembered that I had yet to meet the family we had eagerly awaited at the airport. I left my bed, curious to see if anyone else was awake, but the house lay quiet. Reluctant to return to sleep, I sat at the edge of my bed, patiently awaiting the awakening and departure of others from their chambers. After a while, I discerned the faint voices of children, which was unusual to hear, and I started straining to catch snippets of their conversation.

Although I could discern the English language, the peculiar manner in which they spoke rendered it difficult to comprehend their dialogue fully. Their English seemed unfamiliar, unlike anything I had encountered before, leaving me perplexed. Eventually, my curiosity got the better of me, despite my initial shyness around new faces. I finally summoned the courage to step out and follow the sound of the unusual voices to the dining room, where two young children were discussing something animatedly. Coming from a culture of soft-spoken individuals, the volume at which they conversed bewildered me—was this their customary manner or mere enthusiasm?

Although I struggled to grasp the entirety of their conversation, I observed them for a few moments, their unfamiliar faces captivating my attention. They lowered their voices respectfully upon seeing me, and one of them greeted me with a warm hello. I noticed that I was only slightly older than them—a rarity within our household. Circumstances had led me to spend a couple of Christmases with my aunt's side of the family, but this time, I had returned to my grammy's side. Perhaps this prompted their curiosity in getting to know me.

The young boy inquired about my name. English was my second language, but the dialect he employed was unlike any I had encountered. I managed to discern the word "name." Keen not to appear ignorant, I shared my name and inquired about theirs. The boy introduced himself as Fred, while the girl identified herself as Eve. As I evaluated whether they understood my English proficiently, a sense of unease lingered. I dreaded the prospect of facing a second question I couldn't comprehend. I contemplated retreating to my room but couldn't think of a good excuse to do so. Fortunately, one of my aunts showed up, enabling me to run from potential embarrassment in the presence of these little strangers.

As I got ready for the day, I couldn't shake off my curiosity regarding the peculiar English spoken by the children. I pondered whether this was the language of the outside world or simply a result of their tender age, causing their English to be somewhat garbled and difficult for me to comprehend. I was eager to unravel this mystery but nervous about whether to rejoin Fred and Eve for a conversation. To be honest, I wasn't particularly inclined to do so, but hunger gnawed at my stomach, and the absence of any food in my room left me with no other options. Reluctantly, I made my way back to the dining room. Expecting to find only the people I had left behind, I was taken aback by the sight that greeted me. The room was now bustling with activity, and almost the entire family had gathered. Among the crowd, I noticed two more unfamiliar faces.

Wishing to be polite, I greeted everyone as I made my way through the crowd, heading toward the new faces. One of them, curious, inquired if I was Derrick, to which I nodded in affirmation. She introduced herself as Aunty Sarah and mentioned that she had heard quite a lot about me. I was taken aback by this revelation, as I knew nothing about her, yet she seemed familiar with my name. Aunty Sarah's curiosity about me seemed insatiable, and she bombarded me with inquiries, leaving me momentarily forgetting my own long list of questions. What struck me most was her remarkable ability to speak my mother tongue, Luganda, fluently. Her English was also clear and easily understandable, unlike her children's.

Another fascinating observation was that when Aunty Sarah conversed with her children, her English took on a different tone, which I struggled to comprehend. Intrigued, I raised the issue with other family members nearby, eager to know if they had noticed this too. Before anyone could respond, Aunty Sarah overheard our conversation, chuckled, and moved closer to explain that it was a British accent—a way of speaking used by the British, akin to a distinct language of its own. This revelation opened the floodgates to my endless stream of inquiries about England.

Aunty Sarah proved to be an exceptional storyteller. As she recounted her experiences, I found myself transported to a world I had only dreamed of, vividly imagining the sights and sounds she described. I was enthralled, not wanting her narrative to end. It was as if I were floating in a dreamland where her words were tangible realities. When she finally concluded, all I could think about was how badly I yearned to visit England.

Reluctant to voice my desire aloud and fearing mockery from the rest of the family, I couldn't help but hold off on expressing that until, finally, I joined Aunty Sarah on a walk. She asked about my aspirations and dreams for the future. Without hesitation, I shared my long-standing dream of traveling and becoming a pilot—a recently added dream. Aunty Sarah was supportive, encouraging me to pursue my dreams relentlessly. She also explained that to travel abroad, I would need a few essential elements: a passport, a visa, funds, connections, and plans for accommodation and survival in the foreign country. Initially, it sounded like a daunting and prolonged process, but Aunty Sarah elaborated on the steps involved, making it all seem less impossible than I had initially believed, thanks to the skepticism sown by my cousins.

Intrigued, I asked Aunty Sarah how she managed to stay in England and whether it would be possible for me to join her someday. She expressed no objection, which filled me with immense excitement. It felt as though a door had swung open before me, despite her specific rules should I wish to visit or stay with her in England. Although the rules appeared time-consuming, they seemed attainable. However, one of the primary stipulations was to complete my education, *including finishing college*. That's when I decided that I would need to find an alternative way if I wanted to reach England sooner. Aunty Sarah's plan became my backup, should no other options materialize.

I continued to have several conversations with Aunty Sarah until the season drew to a close and it was time for her and her family to return. I insisted on accompanying them to the airport, and Aunty Sarah was supportive of my wish. When we finally reached the airport and Aunty Sarah bid her farewell, I noticed tears streaming down her cheeks. To my astonishment, some of the family members around us were also emotional. I couldn't fathom why they were crying. As for me, I focused on the ice cream Aunty Sarah had purchased, finding solace in that simple pleasure.

Once we got home, I needed to ensure I wouldn't forget any of the important requirements for overseas travel, so I meticulously wrote them down on a piece of paper. On the list were several key points, such as the need to exhibit good behavior both at home and outside, and the importance of attentively listening to the advice and instructions given by my family. Additionally, my aunty emphasized the significance of finishing college and having a strong willingness to further my studies. This comprehensive list served as a constant reminder of the expectations placed upon me, guiding my actions and decisions as I navigated through life's journey. I tucked it away under my bed. Frequently, I would refer to it, silently praying to God for the means to fulfill my dream. Obtaining a passport was the first step, even though I had no idea where to begin. Nonetheless, my unwavering faith assured me that sooner or later I would acquire one.

~ 7 ~

Passport

As the final days of my primary school education drew near, a mix of emotions stirred within me. In Uganda, primary school includes grades one through seven, and it serves as the foundational level of education before students proceed to secondary school (high school). Initially, I couldn't contain my excitement thinking about the end of early mornings, homework assignments, and exams. The prospect of stepping into a new chapter of my life filled with unknown adventures and opportunities seemed invigorating. However, as the day of primary school graduation approached and I stood amid my fellow graduates, clad in our caps and gowns, a profound realization washed over me that this significant milestone marked the end of an era. I was bidding farewell to the carefree days of childhood and the familiar halls that had become a second home.

As I walked across the stage to receive my diploma, the weight of the moment struck deep within my heart, and I couldn't help but feel a bittersweet ache for the days gone by. The memories flooded back, vivid and cherished. The laughter echoing in the playground, the camaraderie forged during group projects, the innocent friendships with classmates and teachers that blossomed during lunch breaks. These fragments of the past would now be frozen in time, and I would never relive them.

Over the summer, these thoughts gradually transformed into a profound sense of loss. I began to yearn for the innocence and simplicity of those days, when my biggest worries revolved around playground games and spelling quizzes. The years built my character, friendships, and understanding of the world. While the path forward held its own promises and adventures, a part of me would forever remain anchored in those early years that had shaped the person I would become.

High School

Embarking on the journey of high school presented me with a new set of challenges, signaling a significant transition from my primary education. I was faced with a crucial decision: selecting the most suitable high school from a list of four options. Interestingly, my choice was swiftly made when I discovered that my older cousins were attending a specific high school. Their positive experiences and familiar presence influenced my decision greatly, assuring me that I would have a sense of camaraderie and support as I ventured forth. The idea of entering a boarding school environment devoid of any acquaintances had seemed daunting, and I opted for a sense of belonging right from the start.

The list of essentials for my time at the boarding school was comprehensive. I engaged in a comprehensive shopping expedition to acquire all the necessary items, both big and small, that would facilitate my daily life in the dormitory—everything from bedding and school supplies to a lockable trunk or suitcase, laundry supplies, a mosquito net, snacks, and more. I finally stood ready, feeling a mixture of excitement and hope about embarking on this educational adventure.

My high school stood out as one of the prominent institutions in its district, known for its academic excellence and comprehensive facilities. Positioned on a steep slope near the county road, it required a two-hour commute from my house. Before I stepped into my uncle Michael's car, I hugged my grandmother tightly, trying to hide the tears welling up in my eyes. "Don't worry, Grandma, I'll make you proud," I whispered, trying to sound brave. She smiled warmly, her eyes glistening with emotion. "I know you will, my dear," she replied, patting my back affectionately. Aunty Ruth joined the farewell, giving me a tight hug. "Study hard and take care of yourself," she said, her voice filled with love and sadness. "I will," I promised, blinking back tears. The two-hour drive to the boarding school was the quietest journey I had ever experienced. Emotions swirled inside me. The road stretched ahead, mirroring the uncertainty that lay before me. Thinking of the familiar sights and sounds of my neighborhood seemed bittersweet, knowing I would be away from them for a while. Yet at the same time, those thoughts were counterbalanced by the opportunities and adventures that awaited at the boarding school.

I found myself instantly fascinated but overwhelmed by the awe-inspiring grandeur of the school campus. I had never seen such a large educational institution before. Turning to my uncle, I took a deep breath, trying to find my courage. "Thank you for bringing me here," I said, my voice wavering slightly. "Take care of yourself," he replied, giving me a reassuring pat on the shoulder. With one last wave, I walked toward the school entrance, carrying my suitcase and dreams of a brighter future. As I looked back one final time, I saw my uncle standing there, his smiles and love giving me the strength to keep going.

However, as my uncle's car departed, a wave of emotions swept over me, and my tears increased. I was now separated from my family and left to navigate this unfamiliar world alone. My cousins and brother had already settled in their classes, but I looked forward to meeting them after class hours.

The campus buzzed all day with activity as students rushed to and from classes, and I felt a constant mix of nervousness and excitement. Everything was new and unfamiliar, yet I couldn't wait to explore it all. My teachers seemed caring and nurturing, and when the school day ended, I finally reunited with my cousins and brother, and we shared stories of our first day. The joy of being together on my new journey filled my heart with warmth. As the sun set, casting a golden hue over the campus, I knew this boarding school experience would not just be about education; it would be a chance to strengthen our family bonds and create lasting memories together. With their support, I felt more at ease, ready to embrace all that this new chapter had in store for us.

Friends

It was during this formative period that I began forging valuable friendships with my classmates. Some of my peers were also new to the concept of boarding school life, while others possessed prior experience. These newfound friendships provided me with a sense of belonging and acceptance, allowing me to blend into the high school community and navigate the complexities of this transformative period in my life.

One day, while engrossed in conversation with one of my friends, the topic of passports arose. I became intrigued when he casually mentioned that he had recently obtained his passport. Eager to learn more, I inquired about the process he went through to acquire it. To my surprise, he revealed that his uncle, who happened to work at the passport office, had facilitated the entire procedure for him. The news instantly lifted my spirits. I couldn't help but express my desire to speak with his uncle and explore the possibility of obtaining a passport for myself. However, fate had other plans—his uncle's hectic schedule allowed him to be home only on Sundays. Undeterred, I gathered the courage to request my friend's assistance in arranging a meeting with his uncle, hoping he could put in a good word for me. Graciously, my friend agreed to help, unable to deny my heartfelt plea. He assured me that he would convey my request during his next encounter with his uncle. I eagerly set out on the waiting game, eager for any response.

As time ticked by, and days turned into weeks, I began to grow restless with the absence of any news. Doubts started to creep into my mind, questioning whether my friend had truly spoken to his uncle about my situation. However, deep down, I found it hard to believe that my friend would talk with me about passports, agree to help, and then deceive me. After enduring a month of silence without any response, and with it being one of our quarterly term breaks, my patience reached its limit and I decided to pay my friend a visit. I beat around the bush before finally feeling brave enough to ask if he had his passport in his room. To my surprise, he retrieved it from his bedside table, a document adorned with the word "passport." Although I had never seen one before, aside from knowing it was a travel essential, I couldn't contain my fascination. Even though I knew it wasn't mine, I found myself studying every detail, especially his photograph. This sight reassured me and dispelled any lingering doubts about his help. I discovered that my friend had indeed communicated with his uncle. However, due to the uncle's busy schedule, it was uncertain when we would be able to meet. All I could do was keep waiting for his response, which proved frustrating. At times, I even began to entertain the notion that his uncle might not be interested in meeting me, prompting me to consider exploring other avenues. Yet, I remained clueless as to where else to turn. And then my prayer was answered. Unexpectedly, my friend's uncle expressed his desire to meet me the following Sunday evening. I couldn't help but suddenly feel a surge of anxiety. I pondered how to initiate the conversation and interact with someone I had never met. I asked my friend if he would accompany me, hoping to alleviate some of the apprehension.

Initially, my friend chuckled and teased me, asking if I was afraid of his uncle. While fear wasn't the dominant emotion, I confessed that I felt uneasy due to the unfamiliarity of the situation. I hardly knew anything about his uncle beyond his relation to my friend, and this made it challenging for me to feel comfortable initiating a conversation or asking questions. Thankfully, my friend agreed to accompany me, easing my worries. My friend's uncle was engrossed in watching a soccer game on television when we were ushered into the living room. As soon as he noticed our arrival, a smile stretched across his face. My friend had shared a few details about me, leading him to inquire if

I had any imminent travel plans. I responded affirmatively, even though my actual plans were not immediate; nevertheless, I believed it was crucial to take things step by step.

The uncle then began to outline three key considerations for obtaining a passport. First and foremost was the requirement of my guardian's consent since I was still far from reaching the age of eighteen. Additionally, financial costs and paperwork were significant factors to address. However, the enormity of the sum caught me off guard. Obtaining the passport came at a hefty cost of 600,000 UGX, which amounted to approximately 160 USD. At my age, I had never possessed such a substantial amount of money. An overwhelming sense of uncertainty clouded my thoughts, and although I contemplated bargaining or negotiating, my limited familiarity with his uncle restrained me. Consequently, I remained silent. While comprehending the guardian rule also proved challenging, I couldn't envision a way to acquire such a sum, and my mind drifted, unable to focus as he talked. Eventually, he inquired if I still wished to proceed with the passport process. I had no choice but to inform him that I would get in touch once I had gathered the required funds and fulfilled the remaining prerequisites, as I lacked them at that moment.

The uncle displayed great understanding and asked me to inform him when I was ready. When I inquired later about how my friend managed to gather the necessary funds for his passport, he explained that both his parents and uncle had provided him with financial support. In contrast, I had no one to turn to for assistance and I was hesitant to involve my family, fearing their discouragement. Although optimism usually guided me, at that moment I couldn't conceive of any viable options for acquiring the necessary finances. This seemingly insurmountable mountain was obstructing my path and putting my dreams on hold. I felt helpless.

Adding to my dismay, once the school year was over, several school friends and acquaintances departed to reunite with their families overseas. I managed to maintain contact with some of them initially, and I learned about their experiences and sentiments upon arrival in their homes. My only option seemed to be staying in school, but I was restless and resorting to endless prayers, hoping for doors to open.

8

The Trip and a Best Friend

My longing to explore the world beyond my city grew increasingly desperate. By now I possessed a fragmented understanding of what lay beyond, but I yearned to witness and experience it with my own eyes. What helped me satiate this desire were the occasional school-organized but brief excursions to the outskirts of the city. For one trip, my school had something grander in store—an extensive, week-long trip that would take us far from the city. They kept the exact location a mystery, heightening our keenness. The prospect of venturing outside my city's confines stirred up the need for information or guidance, and my go-to confidant was my friend, Boy. Boy had a towering presence, his head standing out among the crowd. Despite his imposing stature, his calm, soft-spoken nature made him approachable. His laughter was infectious, and he had an innate ability to find humor even in the simplest of moments, bringing joy to those around him. But beyond his humor, he was remarkably knowledgeable, possessing a wealth of wisdom that seemed far beyond his years. What struck me the most about Boy was his deep understanding and empathy toward others. He had an uncanny ability to listen intently and offer thoughtful insights without judgment. He genuinely cared about the well-being of those in his circle and was always available to lend a helping hand or a listening ear. A true friend, his presence in my life was a blessing, and his friendship left a lasting impact that I will always cherish.

Though I never discovered the origin behind his moniker, it had stuck with him throughout our friendship. One day I asked Boy, slightly older than me, if he possessed any knowledge of the world beyond Kampala, my city. I had nicknamed him "Google" because he possessed a vast wealth of knowledge that astounded me. I often wondered where he acquired such a breadth of information, as he seemed to know nearly everything I wanted to learn about. Between his generously shared details and the advertisements plastered across every department, I eagerly enrolled for the school trip.

The school trip, I eventually discovered, would span an entire week and involve visiting Queen Elizabeth National Park, situated on the western border of my country. This news ignited my imagination, as I envisioned myself standing at the border and peering curiously into the neighboring country. It became the paramount goal on my list of things to accomplish during this upcoming excursion. Finally, after what felt like weeks of waiting, the day of the trip arrived. I had prepared myself diligently, ensuring I was ready for the adventure ahead. Eager to preserve precious memories, I asked my grandmother if she had a camera or anything I could borrow. Unfortunately, she didn't possess any cameras, but her thoughtful gesture surprised me. She handed me a flip phone with a camera and encouraged me to use it to capture some pictures.

While most of my friends excitedly talked about the opportunity to encounter wild animals within the park, my focus lay on reaching the border to catch a glimpse of lands on the other side of my country. We set off on the school bus early in the morning. Throughout the ride, I intermittently dozed off, only to awaken with a pressing question for my friend: "Have we reached the border yet?" The tantalizing aroma of food wafted from roadside vendors at each stop along the way, tempting me with barbecues and an array of enticing treats. As our journey progressed, I gradually bore witness to the sights Boy had previously described. Leaving behind the plateau on which my city was perched, I marveled at the breathtaking mountains and winding roads snaking their way around them. Exhilaration and trepidation intertwined within me, for I could now glimpse the precipitous slopes leading to the other side. The thought of potentially losing my life before laying eyes on my intended destination weighed heavily on my mind.

Several hours later, we finally arrived at the national park. I found myself particularly surprised when I spotted elephants mere feet away. Never before had I been in such close proximity to these majestic creatures. We ventured farther through the park, observing an abundance of wildlife. Warthogs seemed to grace our presence wherever we went, living freely and displaying a nonchalant demeanor. We explored the diverse vegetation, salt lakes, and countless other natural wonders. The presence of numerous tourists from different countries struck me, highlighting that their knowledge of my homeland far exceeded my own.

As the trip drew to a close, I wondered whether the border visit had been forgotten, until I learned that we would indeed drive by it before departing. Fortuitously, one of the border officers happened to be vacationing at the national park. Upon discovering our status as a school group hailing from a distant region of the country, he expressed his delight at our arrival and offered to facilitate our crossing of the border, assuring us we could explore briefly before departing if we so desired. To my surprise, the entire group erupted in celebration upon hearing this news.

Accompanied by the officer himself, we headed toward the border. His connections with fellow officers expedited their thorough inspection to ensure we carried nothing amiss. Finally, we ventured into a different country. It felt like a surreal dream come true for each one of us. The portion of the Congo I glimpsed from the bus window bore a striking resemblance to Uganda. Verdant landscapes encircled by towering mountains and adorned with lush trees unfolded before us. A hushed silence pervaded the bus as none of us expected or believed we had truly entered a foreign land. Our journey continued for a few hours until we reached a bustling outdoor market.

This vibrant market offered a plethora of items for household needs, ranging from electronics to groceries and clothing. Only when I attempted to purchase a souvenir did I realize the language barrier, as the vendor responded in a tongue completely unfamiliar to me. Confusion set in, compelling me to retreat to the rest of the group. Relaying the incident to them, I discovered that everyone in the market hailed from different countries, hence their use of a foreign language. Just as Boy had previously explained, diverse languages exist across different regions and nations.

As I ventured again through the bustling market, I couldn't contain my excitement. Eagerly, I pulled out my grandmother's phone to capture the vibrant scenes around me. I even began recording a video; however, my joy was abruptly interrupted when a particular man vehemently expressed his displeasure at being recorded in a language foreign to me, unaware that I couldn't comprehend his words. His tirade continued, escalating in volume and intensity. Concerned for my well-being, one of my schoolteachers approached, attempting to decipher the man's outburst. Though unable to understand, he stood by my side, ready to shield me from any harm, and he distanced us from the man's tirade. The bewildering encounter left me shaken.

Throughout the day-long bus journey home, I tried to assimilate all my newfound knowledge and emotions. Eager to share my experiences with family and friends back home, I anticipated their reactions to the tales I would recount. Darkness enveloped the bus as we reached my city. Many opted to spend the night at school, but my eagerness to share overrode any weariness. I promptly hailed a taxi, planning on rushing home to recount the extraordinary journey, but the late hour had lulled the household into slumber. Sleep was elusive for me as I eagerly awaited the morning to share my remarkable adventure with those closest to me. The following day, I groggily awoke after having overslept, only to find myself alone in the house. Seeking to recount my journey to someone, I located Boy and regaled him with the incredible account of our border crossing, which he initially met with skepticism. However, to his surprise, I presented him with irrefutable photographic evidence of our adventure. With that hurdle overcome, I delved into the intricacies of the diverse languages spoken in the neighboring country and the perilous encounter I had with a stranger. Boy, in turn, enlightened me about the existence of other languages within our own country—a revelation that struck me with astonishment, as I had never encountered such linguistic diversity in my city.

My Nation

Boy embarked on a rich discourse about the cultural tapestry that weaved through our nation. Until that moment, my focus had been fixed solely on the allure of the outside world. Yet as he talked, I realized that my own country held untapped wonders and secrets too, challenging me to explore and familiarize myself with the richness within my reach while I awaited the realization of my dreams of venturing beyond its borders. Motivated by this newfound awareness, and though the demands of school necessitated my constant attention, I managed to glean a wealth of theoretical knowledge about my own country, albeit with limited practical exploration.

My friendship with Boy blossomed, fortified by our mutual love for soccer, our fascination with technology and all things innovative, and our passion for computers. He turned out to be an incredibly surprising and fascinating friend. His dedication to research far surpassed mine. Every time we spent a while together, he never failed to amaze me with something new and intriguing. Whether it was his unique perspective on life, his vast knowledge of local traditions, or his adventurous spirit, there was always something to learn from him. Our conversations were filled with captivating stories and insightful discussions that broadened my horizons and opened my mind to new possibilities. Boy's presence in my life enriched it considerably.

9

The Church Tournament and a Cousin

As a devout Christian, my faith journey was deeply ingrained in my life, and I cherished the time I spent attending church every Sunday. The teachings and sense of community in my church provided me with solace and inspiration, and church was a significant part of my upbringing. However, due to being in boarding school, my active involvement in my home church became a bit challenging to maintain consistently. I found myself splitting my time between my home church and the school church, depending on where I was at a given time. Despite this, my faith remained steadfast, and I carried the values I learned from both communities with me, shaping my understanding of spirituality in unique ways. To my surprise I discovered that my friend Boy also shared a similar belief, although he attended a different congregation. I had always known Boy as a devout Protestant, faithfully attending a

Protestant church. However, it wasn't until Boy's church organized a soccer tournament involving other nondenominational churches in the area that I learned about his switch to embrace a nondenominational belief, often referred to as *mulokole* in our local context. Unfortunately, my own church was located in a different region and therefore did not participate in the tournament.

Boy approached me about joining his church soccer team, since they were short on players. He shared the soccer field's address and offered to carpool, ensuring that I wouldn't back out at the last minute. Upon our arrival, we were warmly greeted by Boy's teammates, who I enthusiastically joined, contributing to their victories by scoring multiple goals in different matches. The tournament concluded with joyous celebrations and a sense of camaraderie among the participants.

To my astonishment, some of Boy's church teammates hailed from my neighborhood and had even attended the same elementary school, though they were in higher grade levels. It was a pleasant surprise to cross paths with acquaintances in this new context.

A few days after the tournament and intrigued by Boy's revelation of his beliefs, I expressed my curiosity about his church and the specific denomination he had joined. He graciously explained the unique aspects of worship being more casual and participatory, with an emphasis on engaging the congregation in active worship. Congregants were encouraged to express their faith through singing, clapping, raising hands, and other forms of physical expression. I wasn't a stranger to the inclusive nature of being a nondenominational believer since I was familiar with the denomination. In Boy's warm enthusiasm, he extended an invitation for me to visit his church sometime to experience their faith community firsthand. Eager to explore this new spiritual environment, I agreed, knowing that having Boy by my side would alleviate any apprehension. We set a date for a Sunday visit. Excitedly, I dressed up and accompanied Boy to his church. Upon arrival, I was immediately struck by the stark contrast between Boy's church and my own. My church had an air of grandeur with its sturdy brick walls, iron sheet roof, paved floor, and sleek iron doors, Boy's congregation gathered in a simple, unassuming structure. Crafted from tree poles, wood, and covered with dry papyrus weeds, their place of worship exuded a humble charm. The earth floor was carefully dampened to prevent dust from rising, creating a sense of tranquility and reverence during their gatherings. I couldn't help but be struck by the raw beauty of their simplicity. It was a place where the essence of worship was stripped down to its purest form, away from the materialistic distractions that often permeate modern places of worship. The sense of community and togetherness among the congregants was palpable, with each person actively participating in the worship experience. In that modest sanctuary, I found a different kind of beauty—one that emanated from the shared devotion and genuine connection to their faith. It was a humbling experience teaching me that the true essence of worship lies not in the opulence of a building but in the sincerity of the hearts that gather to seek solace and spiritual nourishment.

Also in the church were familiar faces from the soccer tournament, which instantly made me feel more at ease, despite being in an unfamiliar setting. Boy, being a well-known figure in his church, introduced me to several individuals serving in different ministries. One notable introduction was to his pastor David, who had a commanding presence. Standing tall with a strong build, he exuded an air of authority and confidence. His warm, expressive eyes twinkled with kindness, and his smile was infectious, instantly putting those around him at ease. Despite his height, he moved with gentle grace, and his gestures were always intentional and purposeful. Pastor David wore simple, comfortable attire, opting for a collared shirt and dress pants, which reflected his down-to-earth and approachable nature.

His resonant voice carried well across the congregation during sermons and speeches. When he spoke, I could hear the sincerity and passion in his words, attracting the attention of everyone listening. What stood out the most about Pastor David was his genuine and caring demeanor. He had an innate ability to make others feel valued and understood, and his physical presence reflected the warmth and compassion he carried within. Pastor David warmly greeted me as if we had met before, despite it being our first encounter. I couldn't help but wonder why he spoke to me as though he recognized me. Unbeknownst to me, news of the soccer players who had helped Boy's church team achieve victory had spread throughout the congregation. Many church members were thrilled to meet the players in person, and I realized that more people were aware of my presence than I had thought.

My time spent in Boy's church was thoroughly enjoyable, so much so that I attended it with Boy on several occasions, I formed numerous friendships and relished the opportunity to reconnect with childhood acquaintances who were also part of this congregation. In contrast to my previous church, where I felt like a familiar face in a large crowd, I experienced a deeper sense of connection and belonging within this new spiritual community, prompting me to contemplate the possibility of switching churches. The more services I attended, the clearer the decision to switch churches became. It wasn't just the vibrant worship and inspiring sermons that drew me in, but also the strong sense of camaraderie among the youth in the congregation. Many of them lived close to me, and we quickly formed a bond through shared interests and experiences.

Once I changed churches, having familiar faces around me, especially peers who were navigating similar stages of life, made the transition feel much more natural. We laughed together, supported one another through challenges, and shared our dreams and aspirations. It was a community that embraced diversity and encouraged individual growth, making it an environment where I felt truly accepted and understood. We not only shared similar values and beliefs, but we also shared hobbies and passions. From playing sports together to participating in community service projects, we found joy in activities that brought us closer as friends and as members of a spiritual family. This church provided me with an enriching and supportive environment to deepen my relationship with God and foster lasting friendships that continue to enrich my life to this day.

Town or Country

Over time, I discovered that my new church organized gospel mission trips. One such mission intrigued me greatly—a trip to Togo—but upon questioning Boy about the country, I noticed he made no mention of passports, visas, or air travel. Eventually, I interrupted Boy and posed a direct question: "Are you referring to Togo, the country, or something else when you mention 'Toggo'?" Boy burst into laughter upon my misunderstanding. He revealed that all this time, he had been referring to a town named Toggo in the Ugandan countryside, located approximately three hours away from our hometown. Disappointment washed over me, but despite the mix-up, I still became intrigued to explore this local version of "Toggo."

Fired up for my first gospel mission experience, I eagerly shared my intention to participate in the next Toggo mission with my newfound church community.

Although the exact timing of the trip remained uncertain, I eagerly looked forward to the opportunity to serve God far beyond my comfort zone. While waiting, I received news that my aunt from England was visiting the country. It had been quite some time since we'd last met, so I excitedly made my way to my family's house to reconnect with her. To my delight, my cousin Fred accompanied her once again, though this time he had grown considerably and appeared quite different. Since their previous visit, his transformation had been nothing short of remarkable—he had grown taller, now standing head and shoulders above me. His once lean frame had filled out, reflecting a newfound strength and presence. I couldn't help but notice how his facial features had matured to having a chiseled jawline and a broader smile that lit up his face. Despite these physical changes, his warm personality and confident demeanor remained unchanged. I distanced myself from them, but they noticed.

Curiosity piqued, my cousins approached me and inquired about my aloof behavior. To their surprise, I responded in a more comprehensible manner, as my grasp of English had improved since their last visit. I explained that I had struggled to understand them during their previous stay, assuming it would be the same this time. Their laughter filled the room, realizing that they hadn't realized the communication barrier I had faced. This newfound connection with them, fueled by their amusement at my previous misunderstanding, strengthened our bond.

As days went by, I found myself spending most of my time with my English cousins. They shared fascinating insights about England and highlighted the differences between their home and my city. These conversations were a source of great pleasure for me. Meanwhile, my cousins relished our interactions and expressed their desire for me to visit England someday.

Without hesitation, I eagerly affirmed my desire to visit. They inquired why I hadn't visited them in England yet, prompting me to explain the intricacies of the travel process and its difficulties. In response, my cousins made heartfelt promises to do whatever they could to help make my dream a reality. Their genuine intentions brought a smile to my face, although deep down, I understood that they were just teenagers like me and accomplishing such a journey wouldn't be easy. Nevertheless, I remained optimistic.

Time flew by, and eventually the day came when my cousins had to fly back to England. Each farewell served as a poignant reminder of their ability to travel back and forth whenever they pleased. It struck me hard, for it felt as if they were living the dream I held dear in my heart. I struggled with goodbyes, holding onto the belief that someday God would bless me with the opportunity to explore and see the world beyond my current boundaries. That hope sustained me, even as I bid my cousins farewell.

- 10 -

Gospel Mission

ack at my church, anticipation filled the air as we received more details about our upcoming gospel mission to Toggo. It was a joy to see all my friends at church equally prepared and enthusiastic. However, amid my readiness, I couldn't help but feel a sense of nervousness about what lay ahead.

My backpack became a vessel for essentials like toothbrush, sponge, toothpaste, and clothes. I felt a profound readiness for the mission, even before its official commencement. When my family noticed me packing my belongings, I shared with them that I was embarking on a gospel mission. The desire to spread the message of faith and hope to those in need was the driving force behind my decision to undertake this challenging adventure. Although some of my family members tried to dissuade me, expressing legitimate concerns for my safety, their words did little to shake my resolve. I had a profound sense that this journey was meant to be, and that God's guiding hand was leading me down this path. I bid farewell to my family, knowing I wouldn't be returning home for close to a month.

Teamwork

Our mission group comprised mostly of teenagers—predominantly male—and many of them were my church friends and Boy. To my surprise, our group already had a name: the "Kampala Boys." As we hailed from Kampala city and were venturing beyond its borders, the name resonated effortlessly. We were to work in unity and harmony with our fellow team members from both the local community and the USA—a group of dedicated individuals from the United States who would be joining us in our endeavor. These team members were part of an organization called YAAKA AFRICA, here to partner with us to support and minister to the communities we would visit. Their presence added an extra layer of encouragement. Their willingness to travel thousands of miles to minister alongside us was a testament to the power of faith and the desire to make a positive impact on the lives of others.

We traveled for more than two hours in the back of a truck, speeding along at over seventy miles per hour. Without a windshield at the back, the gusts of wind made it difficult to breathe or hear, forcing me to shield my face with my palms to maintain a steady breath. Tears streamed from my eyes, and I found solace in closing them momentarily. The bumpy road caused my body to lift off the truck with each jolt. In those exhilarating moments, I found myself silently uttering prayers, desperately clutching onto the rails to avoid being thrown off. Leaving the town behind, we ventured onto dirt roads, and a thick cloud of dust enveloped us, obscuring my vision of the surroundings. Swiftly, I reached for my backpack and used it as a shield against the gritty particles and the relentless wind that swept through us on our journey to Toggo.

Arriving in Toggo filled me with an overwhelming sense of excitement. Nestled deep in the Nakaseke district, the town was surrounded by majestic rocky mountains and adorned with lush trees, scattered small-scale forests, and thriving farmlands. The community relied heavily on subsistence farming and hunting, and they had limited access to running water and electricity. Instead, they relied on solar power, as well as traditional lighting sources like candles and lanterns. Boreholes and water wells provided the essential water for their everyday lives.

As we disembarked from the truck in Toggo, I glanced at the faces of my fellow passengers only to find them covered in a layer of dirt. Boy was quick to point it out, and upon touching my own face, I was astounded by the amount of dirt that had accumulated. We couldn't help but laugh, jokingly comparing who had become the dirtiest among us.

Get to Work

During that month, our team set up a stage in a nearby soccer field for the open-air crusades and other events that required a platform, ensuring it faced the ideal direction for optimal visibility and acoustics. To construct the stage, we had to drag precut pine trees to the field from a nearby forest—an arduous task, due to the narrowness and steepness of the trail that stretched over half a mile. We also set up the speaker system, ensuring excellent audio quality for the open-air crusades and children's activities, such as Vacation Bible School (VBS); and we agreed on how we would give soccer and volleyball lessons. We would tear down and set up the same speaker system every day. At the end of the month, we laid the foundation for additional classrooms for a school.

I frequently enjoyed meaningful conversations with the US team. Despite my tendency to be reserved in the company of unfamiliar faces, a member of the USA team, Ferry, astutely observed my reticence and took the initiative to bridge the gap. Her compassionate outreach empowered me to shed my inhibitions, ultimately leading to our enduring bond as best friends.

Evangelism Teams

Although I had never preached or prayed with a group of people before, my spirit blazed with fervor for the Lord, eradicating any traces of fear. With the rest of the US team, we often did door-to-door evangelism.

Divided into groups of three, I was assigned to a group of myself and two Americans on our first evangelism trip, with my role being that of translator. During our conversation, I was taken aback when they remarked that I sounded British. Unbeknownst to me, my frequent interactions my English cousins had led me to subconsciously adopt certain aspects of their accent.

Many of the families in the homes we were welcomed into were excited to see a *muzungu* (White person). Some of the locals even spoke English, albeit with accents divergent from those of the US team. Little children approached us with glee, extending warm greetings to the team from the United States.

Acting as an intermediary, I bridged the linguistic divide. Witnessing both parties' mutual elation upon finally understanding one another brought smiles to all our faces. All the families we visited were very hospitable as we shared the gospel, listened to their stories, and offered prayers. It struck me profoundly that many residents in the northern region were devout Catholics who had never been exposed to the teachings of Jesus Christ. This realization altered my preconceived notions, having grown up in a city where gospel messages were abundant.

Crusade

Each night of the crusade, we harnessed the power of the generator to light up the venue and set the stage for an evening of spiritual awakening. As throngs of people gathered, the atmosphere crackled with expectation. The night commenced with a stirring session of praise and worship, paving the way for the proclamation of the gospel.

As the time for prayer arrived on our first night, an awe-inspiring spectacle unfolded before my eyes—one that defied all my previous experiences. Words fail to adequately describe it all, but I will try. The Holy Spirit manifested his presence, igniting a transformative energy within the crowd. Then the previously subdued sounds of the gathering suddenly erupted into a cacophony of noise. I observed as demons were cast out from tormented souls, their voices simultaneously pleading and exhibiting a disturbing ferocity. People, seemingly possessed by uncontrollable forces, experienced inexplicable manifestations. Some convulsed with a force akin to seizures, their bodies writhing in the grip of an unseen power. Others underwent vocal metamorphosis, their voices taking on an otherworldly quality with an unfamiliar timbre. Yet, amid the chaos, there was an undeniable sense of purpose and release. The atmosphere crackled with a spiritual energy that transcended the bounds of our understanding and blurred the boundaries between the physical and the spiritual realm. While some individuals exhibited violent behavior, it was as if an inner turmoil was being forcibly expelled, making room for healing and transformation and profound moments of spiritual breakthrough and liberation, leaving an indelible mark on the souls of those in attendance.

The healing power of faith transcends our limited human understanding, revealing glimpses of a reality beyond our comprehension—the profound and often mysterious ways in which the divine can work and the immense impact it can have on the lives of those touched. This unfamiliar encounter impacted me on both a physical and emotional level. While I had come across stories of such spiritual battles through radio and television broadcasts, the actual experience left me feeling apprehensive. To ensure the safety of those undergoing intense prayer, we had to intervene and restrain them, safeguarding them from potential harm. In doing so, I found myself inadvertently subjected to physical blows. Kicks, punches, and slaps came my way, to the point when I was overwhelmed by the intensity of the situation. Fear gripped my heart. Time seemed to slow down... but then the miraculous began to unfold. Limbs that had been twisted and contorted straightened with each fervent prayer. Eyes that had been clouded by darkness suddenly sparkled with newfound clarity. The deaf began to hear, and the mute found their voices once again. It was as if the veil between the earthly and the heavenly had been momentarily lifted, and we were granted a glimpse of the boundless power that resided beyond.

Tears of joy flowed freely as individuals were embraced by the tangible presence of healing. Families rejoiced, their shouts of gratitude mingling with the music of the night. The physical healings that unfolded before our eyes were not just isolated incidents; they were powerful demonstrations of the divine love that enveloped us all. In those sacred moments, we were united by a common thread of humanity and faith. The air filled even more with the fervent prayers of those speaking in tongues and the resounding echoes of passionate supplication. The cacophony enveloped the entire space, creating an atmosphere of fervor and devotion. To this day, I find myself reflecting upon the wellspring of strength that propelled me to remain steadfast and committed throughout the entirety of the crusade.

Captivated

Whenever I talked with people from the US team about life in America, their answers unveiled an entirely different way of life, far removed from my own familiar surroundings. Their descriptions of the weather and daily routines shattered my preconceived notions and expanded my perspective. One aspect that particularly fascinated me was the concept of snow, a phenomenon I had previously only encountered through cinematic portrayals. The mere thought of frolicking in the snow fascinated my imagination. However, my excitement waned when I learned that certain parts of the United States experience subzero temperatures. I had never braved anything colder than sixty degrees Fahrenheit. I also learned that the United

States boasts a diverse array of races, dispelling my notion of a single racial majority. I knew I could learn more if I stayed in touch with all my new friends, and we exchanged our contact information over the month.

The last day of the mission dawned, prompting a surge of emotions within the house that had become our shared sanctuary. Reluctantly, we bid adieu to the various individuals who had become our extended family during this transformative period. Tearful hugs were exchanged, and the weight of goodbyes settled heavily upon us. For me even more so as I grappled with the prospect of never crossing paths with certain individuals from the United States again.

During my time on the mission, I bore witness to an extraordinary tapestry of love, miracles, beauty, compassion, and hospitality that defied comprehension. What began as an endeavor to change the lives of others gradually transformed into a personal journey that unveiled more about the Holy Spirit in my life. Prior to embarking on this mission trip, my Christian faith had been confined to Sunday church attendance. However, the experiences I encountered during this life-changing journey sparked a seismic shift within me. I found myself yearning to serve God more deeply and gain a more profound understanding of His divine nature. It was evident that I had to step outside my comfort zone and embrace a new level of devotion and discipleship.

- 11 -

The Promise, Sports, and School

Returning home, the mundaneness of my old life paled in comparison to the vibrant display of missions life I had experienced. I found myself wishing that the exhilaration of mission work could permeate my everyday existence. Thoughts of new destinations consumed my mind, especially when I talked with my newfound friends, seeking their travel advice and recommendations.

As summer drew to a close, the time came for me to return to school. Eager to share my mission experience, I regaled my friends with tales that lingered on my lips. One friend astutely remarked that what I had encountered was akin to traveling, despite being within the same country. To my astonishment, he revealed that he had ventured to a neighboring country by plane, and my experiences mirrored his own. This revelation planted the seed that even journeys within close proximity of home can hold profound transformative power, but I still I reveled in the dreamscape of distant lands. There were moments when I yearned to prolong my slumber, for in dreams I could traverse those uncharted territories.

My Cousin

Time marched on, and my English cousin arrived in the country for Christmas. He requested that I show him around town and we embarked on a spirited exploration of our familiar and hidden gems. When we found a respite in a cozy coffee shop, he broached the topic of my travel aspirations, inquiring about my progress. I sought his guidance on how to speed up my plans. While uncertain about the intricacies of the travel process, he assured me that he had connections who could provide the information and assistance I needed.

Amid the joyous festivities of the Christmas season, my cousin and I reveled in the company of our extended family. As the time neared for his departure back to England, he reaffirmed his commitment to help me escape the confines of Uganda and chase my dreams, wherever they may lead. My cousin and I shared a deep bond, founded on trust and unwavering integrity. His words carried weight, for he was a man of his word who would stop at nothing to fulfill his promises. Even when he returned to England, we maintained constant communication, which kept my dreams alive.

Profound Implications

During that period, my church was once again organizing sports games, and my friends eagerly asked me to join the soccer team. Thrilled by the prospect, I registered and prepared to compete against other church youth groups. The level of competition was fierce, as every church fervently sought victory in their chosen sport. The organization behind the games employed a strategic approach that granted a distinct advantage to the host team, wherein the team responsible for hosting the match would extend an invitation to their adversaries, welcoming them to their own hallowed grounds.

This seemingly simple gesture carried profound implications, for it not only meant stepping onto the field as guests but also navigating the intricacies of an unfamiliar environment. The home team, familiar with every nook and cranny of their turf, possessed an intimate understanding of the terrain, weather conditions, and idiosyncrasies unique to their own grounds, giving them a notable advantage. The home team's players knew which patches of grass were prone to uneven bounces, the optimal angles for long-range strikes, and the subtle slopes that could disrupt a player's balance. Meanwhile, the visiting team found themselves in an entirely different setting, both physically and psychologically. Stepping foot onto the home grounds of their opponents, they were confronted with the unfamiliar sight of grandstands emblazoned with the colors and insignia of the home team's loyal supporters. The very atmosphere exuded an air of unwavering passion and allegiance, a fervor that seemed to echo through the corridors and reverberate in the hearts of the spectators.

Additionally, the support of the home crowd cannot be underestimated. The loyal fans, brimming with unyielding loyalty and unwavering enthusiasm, fill the air with thunderous cheers, chants, and songs. Their vocal presence reverberates across the stadium, fueling the home team's spirit and injecting an electric energy into their every move. The sheer magnitude of their collective voice creates an atmosphere that is both intimidating and inspiring, providing an invaluable source of motivation for the players on the field.

For the visiting team, the weight of the psychological impact of playing in the midst of a fervent home crowd also matters. The pressure to overcome these obstacles and emerge victorious demands exceptional focus, mental fortitude, and adaptability. And yet, true to form, our soccer team emerged triumphant, owing to the exceptional skills of our players, many of whom were actively involved in competitive or recreational leagues. Through these exhilarating victories, I found myself solidifying the bonds we formed through the spirit of healthy competition.

In the wake of the sports competitions, news reached me about an upcoming mission trip on our next summer holiday break. I hesitantly signed up, unsure if I would be available due to my boarding school schedule. Nonetheless, I remained hopeful. Now back for my final year of high school, I made a conscious effort to focus on my studies. I was determined to graduate successfully, and I directed my attention toward completing my high school journey.

Finally, the moment arrived when I donned the graduation gown, ready to bid farewell to high school. The journey to this point had been filled with losses and triumphs. Throughout my high school years, I had immersed myself in my studies, resolved to excel academically. I had poured countless hours into my books, fueled by the desire to make my family proud. Graduation day marked not only the end of a chapter but also a culmination of hard work and dedication, and I felt a profound sense of accomplishment.

Amid the sea of proud parents and good wishes, I scanned the crowd, hoping to catch a glimpse of familiar faces. My family's circumstances meant that not everyone could attend, but a few close friends beaming with pride brought warmth to my heart. Their presence served as a reminder that I was not alone on this journey, that my achievements reflected the support and love that surrounded me. The feeling continued at the celebratory gathering later with school friends. We laughed, reminisced about our high school escapades, and shared our dreams for the future—it was a time to celebrate the achievements we had all worked so hard for.

The holiday that lay before me was a well-deserved respite, a chance to recharge before the next chapter of my life unfolded.

– 12 –

The Loss

With my secondary school education now complete, I stepped through the familiar door of my grandmother's house in a wave of eagerness to experience the heartfelt embraces and shared laughter of my beloved family once again after an extended absence—not only my grandma but also my cousins and beloved aunt. The house felt like a haven of love, togetherness, cherished memories, and strongly woven bonds of family. However, my joy quickly faded when I saw my grandma's deteriorating condition. Several days prior, she had been admitted to the hospital, but her health had continued to decline steadily.

I thought I had mentally prepared myself to see my dear grandma, but she was now robbed of her ability to speak by the relentless grasp of her condition. Instead, my grandmother could only communicate with her eyes whenever someone entered her room. Struck to the core, I faced the stark reality of witnessing her diminished state, shockwaves of distress coursing through every fiber of my being.

The somber atmosphere in the house prevailed, dominated by discussions revolving around my grandma's deteriorating condition. The most heartbreaking moments occurred when we contacted the doctors for updates. Regrettably, their assessments offered little solace: my grandma wasn't doing well, striking me with fear and helplessness. I desperately yearned to do something, but it seemed there was nothing within my power. I fervently offered up prayers in every way imaginable, at times even questioning God, wondering why he would allow such suffering to persist. Yet, despite my doubts, a flicker of faith remained, assuring me that perhaps a miraculous intervention was still possible.

Days passed, but at the age of sixteen, in the early hours of the morning, while preparing breakfast for myself before a planned soccer outing with friends, one of my aunties burst into tears and implored me to call a doctor urgently. Bewildered as to why she hadn't done so herself, I ran toward my grandma's room. It was then that I comprehended why she had been unable to think clearly at that moment.

My grandma struggled to breathe, fighting for her life right before my eyes. Amid my frantic call to the doctor, tears streamed down my face, rendering me almost incoherent on the phone. The doctor requested that I calm down and explain the situation, but my gaze remained fixed on my grandma, and I was paralyzed by a combination of fear and confusion. The words eluded me.

Approximately thirty minutes later, the doctor arrived. Tears flowed ceaselessly from everyone present, prompting the doctor to ask us to vacate the room. After a mere ten minutes, he emerged from the room, beckoning my aunt. They retreated back inside, and upon their return, my aunt's tears persisted. She informed us that the doctor had forewarned us to prepare for the worst. The time had come to bid farewell.

I approached my grandma's room, standing hesitantly in the doorway and observing her valiant struggle for each breath. I longed to express countless sentiments but found myself incapable of doing so. Fear prevented me from drawing closer, even to utter my final goodbye. Departing the house, with tears cascading down my cheeks, I found solace in the earth beneath me, and I beseeched, "My God, my grandma needs your divine intervention."

An hour later, my aunt sought me out and whispered, "Derrick, Grammy is gone." Time seemed to halt. I stood frozen, trying to absorb her words. She continued, "Did you hear me?" but I was in a state of numbness. It felt surreal, yet undeniably real. My aunt persisted in urging me to come and witness it for myself. Grammy had ceased to breathe. I felt lost, unsure of what to do. In my distress, I questioned if another call to the doctor would be of any avail.

Seeking refuge in my room, I locked myself away, yearning to avoid the sight, sound, and voices of those engulfed in sorrow. I was adrift, trying to come to terms with the magnitude of losing my grandma. As my family grew increasingly concerned about my well-being, they implored me to open the door, fearing I might harm myself in seclusion. Eventually, they resorted to breaking down the door, only to find my mind consumed by thoughts of how I would cope without my beloved grammy. During those agonizing hours, my heart felt devoid of its beat.

As plans for the funeral commenced, news of my grandma's passing spread, prompting friends to extend their condolences, visit, and provide much-needed consolation and support. I observed the unfolding events as if from afar. Amid it all, my mind remained preoccupied with thoughts of life without my grandma. Finally, the moment arrived when I had to bid my final farewell. Approaching her casket, I struggled to summon the courage to draw closer, for I yearned to remember her with a smile on her face.

The somber farewell that unfolded over the course of a week and several days marked the end of a poignant chapter. Her body had found its final resting place. The weight of grief, however, proved to be an unwavering companion in the wake of this profound loss. The path to recovery loomed ahead, an arduous journey filled with uncharted emotions and daunting challenges.

In an attempt to find solace amid the tumultuous sea of sorrow, I sought refuge in various diversions. Engaging in exhilarating sports, immersing myself in the virtual realms of video games, embarking on soul-stirring hikes, and seeking solace in the company of cherished friends were all endeavors aimed at escaping the clutches of grief. Yet, despite the temporary respites these activities provided, they proved to be mere ephemeral distractions in the face of the profound void left by her departure. Every evening, the weight of her absence became even more palpable. In the stillness of the night, as shadows danced upon the walls, the hushed echoes of memories resurfaced, mingling with the haunting silence that permeated the once-vibrant abode. Each creaking floorboard, once a testament to her vibrant spirit, now echoed with a mournful cadence.

It was during these solitary moments that fear, like an uninvited guest, stealthily tiptoed into the recesses of my mind, intensifying the ache in my heart and threatening to consume the fragile threads of hope that held me together. Though vulnerable in this darkness that overshadowed my world, glimmers of resilience and hope emerged. In the depths of my despair, I discovered the strength to confront the fears that gnawed at my soul. Through introspection and self-reflection, I realized that healing would not be found in escapism but in acknowledging and embracing the pain, allowing it to shape me into a person capable of navigating the complex labyrinth of grief. And then a glimmer of hope emerged in the form of an unexpected opportunity. My church friends reached out to me with a life-changing proposition.

Determined

They extended a heartfelt invitation for me to join them on a mission trip planned for the following week, during which I could serve others in need. It also offered the camaraderie of my compassionate church friends and a much-needed respite from the grief-laden, familiar surroundings of home. With a mix of anticipation and trepidation, I eagerly embraced the chance to embark on this meaningful journey.

The trip was set to take us to a region where poverty and hardship were prevalent, and we would be carrying out various outreach activities: from providing support to the underprivileged to participating in community-building projects. This prospect filled my heart with a renewed sense of purpose, as I knew that in reaching out to others, I might find healing for my own wounded spirit.

Throughout this period of mourning, a stranger's approach took me completely by surprise. She revealed herself to be my older sister from my mother's side—a branch of the family with whom I had never shared a close connection. The encounter with Patricia, residing in London, held a bittersweet intrigue. Memories of my mother remained veiled in the depths of my mind, her face unfamiliar and her presence merely a distant echo. Patricia's unexpected appearance stirred a yearning in me to discover more about this long-lost part of my family. Her genuine efforts to reach out and make a connection amid my mourning touched me deeply, reflecting the strength of even unknown family ties. As our conversation unfolded, I felt a mix of emotions—pain over the loss of my mother, curiosity about my sister's life in London, and the desire to understand the intricate tapestry of my family's story. We promised to stay in touch, holding the promise of a future where familial bonds could be nurtured and strengthened. Patricia's presence added a new dimension of hope to my life—a glimmer of light amid the shadows, reminding me that even in times of mourning, love and connection could transcend the boundaries of time and distance.

- 13 -

Gomba and Togo Missions

M y family and I embarked on the journey of adapting to our new reality. However, it was far from enjoyable, as we attempted to maintain an illusion of normalcy despite the underlying struggles. Fortunately, the time for the mission trip arrived, bringing a sense of relief that I wouldn't have to remain confined at home any longer.

This mission trip was organized by Kampala Church and a US missionary group from YAAKA Africa. We were to go with a group from Kampala— preachers and a whole group of people connected to Kampala church. This mission trip had a different nature compared to the previous one. We were informed to pack for rain, and we were going to camp in a remote location, adding an element of intrigue to the adventure.

Unlike before, I carefully packed a backpack with only the essentials that I needed. I was happy to learn that we had traded the truck for a van this time, as we would be traveling through vast stretches of dirt roads. .. until we embarked on the journey and discovered the problems it presented. After driving for an hour on these roads, I longed to stretch my cramped legs, but stopping in the midst of the rising dust was discouraged. The situation became so intense that even the driver struggled to see the path ahead. We were compelled to close all the windows to shield ourselves from the swirling dirt, and we continued for approximately thirty minutes, enduring the heat in the van with a broken AC. Finally, we reached a point where we could disembark from the dusty road, and a collective sigh of relief accompanied our desperate gasps for fresh air. After a few minutes of stretching and regaining composure, we reentered the van, continuing toward our final destination.

Our ultimate goal was a quaint town nestled in the countryside named Gomba. By the time we arrived, dusk was approaching, casting a soft glow over the landscape. Our campsite was an open soccer field, where we had to set up our tents before darkness descended. Despite our weariness from the journey, we tackled the task at hand, road dust still clinging to our faces and hair.

Once again, our primary task for the day was to set up the stage, sound systems, and lighting for the evening's open crusade.

During the setup process, the support we received from the local church members near the area was truly tremendous, making the whole task much more manageable. By lunchtime, we had completed the construction of the stage, and the majority of the sound equipment was all set for action.

As evening descended upon us, the team from the United States, whom we had not yet met, joined our gathering. Familiar faces from previous missions were also present, and our smiles illuminated the group as we engaged in heartfelt conversations and final preparations for the crusade program. With the generator switched on once again, the music played, creating an electric atmosphere before the start of the crusade. Starting with praise and worship, we dove into the Word of God and then concluded with hours of intercession while miracles of healing and transformation unfolded before my very eyes, surpassing anything I had ever imagined.

During the daytime, we continued our mission by holding conferences and organizing VBS activities for the children. Nurturing their spiritual growth throughout the week was a rewarding experience, and their enthusiasm and joy left a lasting impact on our hearts.

However, the crusade experience also brought with it various struggles. Living far from the comforts of home, sleeping under the stars in my tent atop the outdoor stage, and being exposed to rain and cold nights were not easy tasks. Yet, amid these trying conditions, I discovered a newfound sense of resilience and trust in God, realizing that material possessions like a television or a phone were inconsequential compared to the spiritual growth and profound connections I was forging during this incredible journey.

Overall, the crusade in Gomba was an unforgettable and life-changing experience, filled with moments of spiritual revelation, communal joy, and personal growth. It taught me more about the power of faith, the beauty of fellowship, and the profound impact of coming together as one united body in Christ.

After the eventful week and a half, it was time to wrap up and prepare for the next phase of the mission in Toggo. I had formed close bonds with new friends from the mission group, including those from the United States and Kampala, as well as the people from Gomba. I yearned for more time in Gomba, but the clock dictated that it was time to move on.

Toggo

Avoiding the congested main roads, we opted for a two-hour shortcut along a dirt road in a truck. Our aim was to travel swiftly, ensuring no car raised dust ahead of us, as we had experienced this worst-case scenario before. Holding on tightly to the truck, we had to navigate the rough terrain while shielding ourselves from the swirling dirt and branches along the road. Attempting to protect our faces from the dust, we used items of clothing as makeshift veils, although the speed at which we were moving rendered this measure ineffective.

Despite the unpleasantness, we eventually reached Toggo, our bodies a uniform shade of brown, with red eyes blending into the mix. The vehicles were coated in dirt, and water became the solution to everything as everyone hurried toward the nearest water source. After freshening up, we unpacked and took some well-deserved rest. Strangely, my voice had undergone a slight change, possibly due to the dust or my efforts to be heard amid the commotion at the back of the truck.

Allergies plagued most of the group that had traveled in the truck. Colds were rampant. However, despite feeling under the weather, we still indulged in board games late into the night. The next day, we teamed up and headed to the school in Toggo, offering our assistance to the teachers with various activities, including sports competitions, Bible studies, cleaning, and painting the school buildings.

Before my first visit to Toggo, I had heard unsettling stories about the town's infestation of jigger fleas. To ward off the fleas, I made sure to never walk barefoot and diligently kept my feet covered and clean. However, my love for soccer occasionally led me to let my guard down, relishing the excitement of playing barefoot after switching from my soccer cleats to my converse shoes ... to my detriment. A jigger flea got into my big toe and laid an egg sac, which my friends graciously removed—making an incision with a sharp razor to extract the egg sac. I tightly shut my eyes, enduring one of the most excruciating pains I had ever experienced, but the flea and its eggs were gone.

In the subsequent days, we spent a lot of time entertaining the children, including hiking and organizing sports, music, dance, and drama competitions. The school was abuzz with excitement, and everyone rooted for their favorite group to emerge victorious. Additionally, I took on the role of translator, facilitating communication between some kids and members of my American group. Witnessing their understanding and the resulting smiles brought me immense joy.

On Sundays, we divided ourselves and visited various churches in different towns to preach, offer encouragement, and support others. As the mission drew to a close, we began bidding farewell to the children and friends we had made along the way. Emotions ran high, and on the eve of our departure, we organized a bonfire, gathering to celebrate the collective efforts and say our goodbyes to the team from the United States, Kampala, and the surrounding areas.

Pastor Hahn

I had met a diverse array of individuals, each weaving their own distinct thread into the rich tapestry of my experiences. Yet one figure emerged as a luminous beacon, casting a warm glow upon the landscape of my heart and memory—Pastor Lance Hahn. His presence etched an indelible mark upon my life, leaving a profound imprint that continues to resonate with me.

What truly set Pastor Lance apart was his profound humility and unwavering devotion to his faith. His love for God radiated from within, illuminating the lives of those fortunate enough to cross his path. His actions spoke volumes, reflecting his genuine care for the well-being of others. Whether it was his unassuming gestures of kindness or his willingness to lend a listening ear, his humility and selflessness created an atmosphere where individuals could flourish and grow, fostering a sense of community that extended far beyond the boundaries of our interactions.

He embodied the very essence of Christlike love—it was palpable, a fire that ignited the spirit and kindled a deep sense of connection to the divine. In his presence, I felt a remarkable sense of comfort and acceptance, as if his very being exuded the gentle embrace of God's grace.

As we talked together and shared moments of reflection, Pastor Lance's wisdom and insight flowed effortlessly. His words were not just a collection of sentences; they were also vessels of profound truth and compassion. Through his guidance, I gleaned a deeper understanding of my own faith journey, and his encouragement bolstered my resolve to embrace the lessons that lay ahead.

Pastor Lance Hahn's presence was a divine gift, a reminder that even in the midst of unfamiliar places and challenging circumstances, there are beacons of light that guide us along the path of our own spiritual odyssey.

– 14 –

Moving

When I finally returned home after the mission trip, I stepped back into a house still cloaked in grief yet even more silent, as some of my cousins had moved away. The weight of loss pressed upon me once again. Every corner of home now reminded me of my late grandma, and the memories overwhelmed me. The pictures on the wall, her favorite spot in the living room, and the echoes of her words and jokes resounded in my ears. Feeling unable to bear the weight of grief, I began to feel consumed by depression. I confided in one of my closest friends about my situation, who was deeply moved. He resided just a short distance away from my previous home and generously invited me to move in with him, Without hesitation, I accepted.

Moving out, Moving On

Moving in with my friend brought a sense of relief, lifting a significant burden from my shoulders. Although I occasionally visited my family, living with my friend became a turning point in my life. It allowed me to grow and focus on my future, guiding me away from the endless cycle of grieving. Instead of dwelling on the pain, I began asking myself crucial questions about what lay ahead. My friend assisted me in finding a job in a computer shop and planning for college. This pushed me out of my comfort zone, propelling me to lay down plans and seek God's guidance, trusting that his will would align with my aspirations.

I found solace in my faith, dedicating more time to reading the Bible and nurturing my relationship with God. I rediscovered my passion for soccer and made new friends within the close-knit community of the smaller, quieter town I had relocated to. It was a place of peace, and I felt a strong connection to one of the soccer teams I joined.

In the midst of settling into my new life, I reached out to my sister Patricia, and we began to build a relationship. Despite living in London, she expressed a genuine desire to get to know her siblings better. I was touched by her interest in me, and she eagerly wanted to bridge the gap between us. One day Patricia revealed that she would be delighted if I would consider joining her in London someday. Her desire to have family close to her made sense, and I enthusiastically agreed. She encouraged me to obtain a passport, assuring me that she had connections to assist us with the process. I couldn't contain my excitement, envisioning the realization of my dreams arriving sooner than expected.

To my surprise, my roommate had connections that could facilitate the passport application. Through his assistance, I initiated the necessary steps, contacting Patricia to update her on my progress. Unfortunately, she never responded. Days turned into weeks, until a year later I finally had the opportunity to see her again, albeit briefly. When I finally built up the courage to ask her about it, I sensed her discomfort and unease. She seemed to brush off my questions, evading any concrete answers, leaving me with a lingering sense of confusion and frustration. Realizing that pressing further might escalate tensions, I decided to let the matter rest and tried to forget about it. Even now, the question of what truly happened remains unanswered.

New Experiences

I encountered numerous challenges while adapting to my new environment at my friend's place. At one point, I fell in with the wrong crowd, enticed into the world of politics due to its material benefits. It seemed appealing, as I gained positions and made new acquaintances. However, as time went on, I realized the price I had to pay. I lost some of my closest friends due to my affiliations with a different political group, prompting me to reevaluate my choices and eventually distance myself from politics altogether.

After stepping away from the political scene, I started attending a different church during the week due to its proximity. It was there where I first heard about an apostle from a friend. Although I had always been skeptical of fortune-tellers and prophets, my friend's persuasive nature led me to agree to accompany him to meet this apostle one day. Arriving at the designated location, I expected to find a church, but instead, we were directed to someone's house. Uncertainty crept in, and I almost reconsidered. However, once the door opened, there was no turning back. I introduced myself to the host and asked a few questions, but my doubts loomed large. However, I voiced my desire to be prayed for, since I was already present. The three of us joined in singing praise songs, and as we began to pray, she urged us to focus solely on God.

Following the prayer, she approached me, held my hands gently, and inquired about my deepest desires. Without hesitation, I shared my dream of exploring the outside world. Her response struck a chord deep within me: "God is capable of granting your every request, but seek first his kingdom, and all else will be added unto you." Her words prompted a shift in my perspective. I began to ponder her wisdom while she resumed praying. For the next few minutes, she continued to intercede on my behalf, all the while maintaining her grip on my hands. With unwavering intensity, she looked deep into my eyes and began unveiling secrets of my past. She revealed events and experiences known only to me, exposing a depth of knowledge that astounded me. Finally, she disclosed my dream of skyscrapers and assured me that it would come to pass in due time.

The surreal experience left me speechless and filled with a mix of awe and trepidation. I couldn't help but question whether my friend had disclosed personal details to her, but the revelations she shared were beyond his knowledge. She conveyed that God keeps his promises and encouraged me to watch as they unfolded.

On the way home, my friend asked for my thoughts, but I found myself at a loss for words. The woman had unraveled the intricacies of my past, leaving an indelible impression. A whirlwind of thoughts consumed my mind as I contemplated the prophecy she had shared. While I had numerous connections in the UK and initially believed it would be my destination if I were to travel abroad, her words about God sending me to the United States persisted. Though it seemed improbable, I harbored unwavering faith in God's ability to make a way.

I continued to interact with the woman, meeting her on several occasions to pray. However, she never prophesied to me again. Nonetheless, her words remained etched in my memory, and I heeded her call to prepare myself for the journey ahead.

– 15 –

Love and Kenya

uring that period of eager anticipation and uncertainty, while awaiting the fulfillment of the prophecy, my involvement in Kampala church remained active. I eagerly participated in numerous gospel missions, consumed by a burning hunger and passion to serve God. What had once been challenging work during my initial mission trips now felt like second nature. I became so focused on the Lord that I hardly noticed the difficulties anymore.

I frequently questioned whether I was doing enough for the Lord, and I even had my first major crush on an American girl, Okzana. What particularly attracted me was her unique charm, a blend of charisma and humility that was both captivating and endearing. It was as if she had an effortless ability to connect with those around her, making everyone feel welcome and appreciated in her presence. But I worried about saying the wrong things and driving her away, so I let my fear stop me from taking my chances and discovering her true feelings. I still wonder how she's doing.

Ferry

Of all the friendships I'd formed with American friends I'd met both within and outside the context of gospel missions, one particular friend stood out. Ferry had previously joined our mission trips, and we had developed a close friendship. She was the first person from the American team whom I had truly connected with. Being an introvert amid a sea of unfamiliar faces, I appreciated how she helped me break out of my shell, and I trusted her enough to share almost everything about myself.

Ferry later returned to Uganda as a teacher with a different organization, which is when she reached out to me. She taught at a prestigious school deep in the countryside, a government institution that was well-known for its rich academic history. She mentioned she occasionally visited my town when she wasn't teaching—an unexpected revelation—and when she expressed a desire to meet up some time, I eagerly embraced the opportunity. Time passed, and one day, Ferry invited me to her upcoming birthday party. However, the location was a two-and-a-half-hour drive away from me, in a town called Jinja. Despite having visited Jinja as a child on a school tour, I felt unfamiliar with the place since it had been quite some time.

Considering my lack of familiarity, I decided it would be best not to go alone. I asked Ferry if I could bring someone along, and she had no objections. Immediately, I thought of my friend Boy, an outgoing individual who would be up for an adventure. Her enthusiastic acceptance was unsurprising. When the much looked forward to weekend arrived, we boarded a bus to Jinja. I had assumed Boy was familiar with the area. However, to my dismay, after the bus had driven us for about three hours and a few minutes, I noticed people speaking a language I couldn't understand. It was then that the driver informed us that we had passed Jinja some time ago and suggested we take another bus back to our intended destination.

After alighting from the bus, Boy and I couldn't help but burst into laughter, playfully blaming each other for the oversight, but we were determined to make it to Jinja and, we quickly hopped on another bus back to our desired destination. Unfortunately, when we arrived at the venue, we found that most of the guests had already departed and only a small group remained. Undeterred, we joined the gathering, using the short time we had left to catch up on life. Since we needed to catch a bus back to Kampala, we reluctantly bid farewell to the party. Fortune favored us though— someone at the gathering said he was heading back to Kampala and generously offered us a ride.

Following Ferry's birthday celebration, our bond grew stronger than ever. We began spending more time together, introducing her to various places in Kampala. Additionally, I made a weekly pilgrimage to Jinja, relishing moments at the riverside with Ferry's local friends and those who had ventured to experience the beauty of Jinja.

Adventures in Kenya

During this period, the friend I was staying with received a remarkable opportunity at his workplace— an invitation to travel to Kenya for a week. Kenya, one of Uganda's neighboring countries in the east, beckoned with its charm. Serendipitously, one of his colleagues had fallen ill and couldn't go, leaving an extra ticket. Seizing the moment, my friend casually asked me if I'd be interested. My heart leaped with joy at the mere suggestion. It was an extraordinary dream come true—one that seemed too good to be real, yet it was happening.

Despite traveling by road rather than air, my enthusiasm remained undeterred. We set off in the middle of the night, embarking on an arduous bus ride that would span nearly eighteen hours. By the time we arrived in Kenya's bustling capital of Nairobi, the sun had painted the sky with its radiant hues, signaling a new day. Exhausted, we slept for the next twelve hours or so in our hotel, and the following morning, we eagerly ventured into the vibrant streets of Nairobi and its surrounding cities. It was a mesmerizing and awe-inspiring experience to be in one of Africa's largest and most influential metropolises. Navigating through Nairobi's bustling streets demanded patience due to the labyrinth of traffic.

The next day, while my friend attended a work conference, I decided to venture to a renowned beach called Diani. There, amid the crowd, I realized that the language being spoken resonated with echoes of my mother tongue, albeit with intriguing variations. Pleasantly surprised and curious, I asked one of the security personnel about the language, and he enlightened me that it was Swahili.

Throughout the remainder of the week, we embarked on further explorations, relishing the opportunity to learn about distinct cultures and draw comparisons between our beloved countries—Uganda and Kenya. Admittedly, I struggled with the unfamiliar cuisine initially, but as I gradually acclimated, I discovered delightful flavors and realized that some dishes mirrored those of my homeland, albeit with different names. Understanding and navigating the local culinary landscape proved to be a fulfilling endeavor. I was also enamored by the westernized aura of Nairobi.

Returning from Kenya, I found myself incredulous that I had ventured to a different country for the very first time. While I had previously visited Congo, it had only been along the border, making this journey a remarkable milestone. Even though Kenya was not an overseas destination, it signified a significant step forward,

- 16 -

The Decision and Visa

Upon my return from Kenya, Ferry and I continued to maintain our close friendship, spending most weekends together. However, I began noticing a shift in her behavior—she showered me with increased attention and care, and an endless stream of deep, probing questions. Initially, I attributed it to our long-standing friendship and her desire to know me better. Little did I know that these were the signs leading up to a significant revelation.

It all unfolded when Ferry started delving into inquiries about my love life, gradually building up to the ultimate question: whether I found her attractive. It was a moment that caught me off guard. Ferry was not just a close friend but also someone who knew and understood me on a profound level. While I couldn't figure out my true feelings for her at that very moment, I was hesitant to jeopardize our friendship by uttering a negative response.

Requesting some time, I made it clear that I needed to contemplate my emotions before providing an answer. Ferry graciously understood and granted me the space I required. Yet, the decision I faced proved to be one of the most challenging of my life, as Ferry held an irreplaceable place in my heart, and any response I gave would inevitably impact our lives. Honesty was paramount, and I resolved not to deceive her by feigning affection I didn't genuinely feel. It was a matter of respect for both her and me. Seeking guidance, I turned to trusted confidants, including my roommate and Boy, hoping they could help illuminate the path before me. To my surprise, they offered counsel but left the ultimate decision in my hands. With Ferry eagerly awaiting my reply, I found myself facing a swirling confusion of conflicting emotions— unable to discern whether the affection I felt was merely a deep friendship or something more profound.

After days of contemplation, I concluded that embarking on dates with Ferry might provide the clarity I sought. With honesty as my guide, I mustered the courage to express my uncertainty, assuring her that while my feelings remained ambiguous, I was willing to embark on this journey together and discover where it would lead. Thankfully, she agreed.

Before our first official date, an unexpected phone call from my cousin in England delivered incredible news. He revealed that he had enlisted the aid of a lawyer to facilitate my relocation to England, kickstarting the process of obtaining the necessary documents. This revelation filled me with boundless excitement, as it opened a realm of new possibilities.

Ferry and I embarked on a couple of dates, one of which took us to an enchanting island in the midst of Uganda's deepest lake, Lake Bunyonyi. It was my first time on an island, and the experience proved to be nothing short of magical. The island offered breathtaking vistas and a sense of serenity. We secured accommodation in one of the most incredible dormitories, affording us a magnificent view of the lake. As someone who appreciates the wonders of nature, this experience was deeply fulfilling. During our time on the island, we made new friends, although I couldn't help but notice that I was the only person of African descent among the visitors. This unfamiliarity stirred a sense of curiosity, momentarily causing me to question if I was still in Uganda. Nevertheless, we reveled in delicious cuisine, engaged in lively games, and Ferry even took a plunge into the lake's depths while I admired the island's beauty, embraced the gentle breeze, and savored the fragrance of the surrounding trees.

While on our island adventure, Ferry playfully inquired about my experience of traveling by plane, to which I admitted I had never flown before. Her subsequent question—whether I harbored a desire to do so—elicited laughter from me. I shared my long-held dream of exploring foreign lands, flying across borders, and discovering what lay beyond. Unfazed by the obstacles I faced, such as lacking a visa, an incomplete passport application, and limited funds or connections, Ferry expressed her willingness to make my dream a reality.

Without hesitation, she produced her laptop, and together we researched destinations that a Ugandan could venture to without a visa. While most neighboring countries posed visa requirements, we stumbled upon Rwanda, which piqued Ferry's interest due to recommendations from her friends. She proposed a trip there, and with my unwavering passion for travel, I wholeheartedly embraced the idea. However, due to Ferry's plans to visit her family in the States for Christmas, we postponed our journey to a later date.

As I observed Ferry deep in thought, I couldn't help but inquire what she was thinking about. Ferry's eyes met mine, and she couldn't resist asking if I would be interested in visiting the United States. Momentarily taken aback by the sudden suggestion, I wondered about the motives behind it. With a mix of curiosity and skepticism, I voiced my surprise and sought an explanation for her intriguing proposal. Ferry, with a warm smile, began to unravel the reasoning behind her invitation, revealing a compelling perspective that gradually piqued my interest.

She painted a vivid picture of the experiences awaiting me on American soil, emphasizing the uniqueness and wonder of spending Christmas in the United States. The appeal of vibrant festivities, cultural diversity, and cherished traditions unfolded before my eyes, igniting a flicker of excitement within me. Ferry's words carried the enthusiasm of someone who had experienced the joy and enchantment of a holiday season in America firsthand. Yet, as my heart yearned to embrace this opportunity, I couldn't help but recall cautionary tales shared by friends and family members who had faced setbacks during their attempts to obtain US visas—arduous paperwork, nerve-racking interviews, and the crushing disappointment of visa denials due to unforeseen or unmet requirements.

Voicing my doubt and trepidation to Ferry, I was astonished to discover that she, too, had heard similar stories from her own circle of friends. The realities of the visa application process were not lost on her. However, she invited me to consider the value of stepping outside the boundaries of others' experiences. She emphasized the notion that embarking on this endeavor, even with the knowledge that failure was a possibility, could bring invaluable personal growth, resilience, and a renewed sense of self. Her words held profound truth—a reminder that taking risks and embracing the unknown can sometimes yield the most rewarding experiences.

The United States beckoned to me, whispering promises of adventure, cultural immersion, and unforgettable memories. A seed of purpose had been planted, fueled by Ferry's encouragement. Would I succumb to fear and doubt or embrace the transformative power of possibility? The decision remained in my hands, a crossroads where my own desires collided with the realities of the world.

Still, I had reservations about finances. To my surprise, Ferry reassured me that finances should not be a concern, as she would take care of them. However, I felt a sense of guilt about that. I couldn't fathom going through the entire process relying solely on her support and potentially facing a visa denial. Attempting to dissuade her, I realized that Ferry had made up her mind, and she remained resolute in her decision. After our conversation, she contacted the American embassy in Uganda to acquire detailed instructions for the visa application process.

Thus, we shifted our focus back to planning our trip to Rwanda, finalizing dates that aligned with her return from the States. That very night, we eagerly booked our tickets. Once back in Kampala, I was overwhelmed with joy by my roommate's news—the long-awaited passport was finally ready, courtesy of his friends. I recognized the hand of God and his alignment of circumstances, and wasted no time in picking up my passport.

Visas

Soon after, my English cousin informed me that he would soon be flying to Uganda, equipped with all the necessary paperwork to facilitate my relocation to England. These continuous developments solidified the realization that my dreams were on the brink of coming true. Yet, amid these extraordinary occurrences, I faced a significant dilemma—deciding between pursuing a future in the United States or the United Kingdom. While the presence of numerous family members in the UK made it an enticing option, my relationship with Ferry complicated matters, as relocating to the UK was not something she would entertain.

When I shared the news of my passport with Ferry, she promptly initiated the process of signing me up for a US visa application online. Together, we completed the form, meticulously entering the details from my passport. However, I discovered an error related to my age, realizing that I had been mistakenly recorded as older than my actual age, which required rectification. Given the urgency of the visa application, I had no time to spare for passport corrections. Thus, I made the difficult decision to proceed with the information as stated in my passport.

After submitting the application, we scheduled an interview date, which was two months away. In the lead-up to the interview, I immersed myself in research, watching online videos to prepare. Although I felt confident and well-prepared, anxiety consumed me as the day approached.

Interview Time

On a rainy and chilly morning, Ferry accompanied me to the American embassy. Despite being an American citizen herself, she was told she could only enter if she had an interview or an appointment with the embassy.

While she waited for me at a nearby restaurant, I walked through security with my documents, nervousness and trembling taking hold. Inwardly, I prayed, surrendering to God's will and acknowledging that this was a significant moment in my life.

After passing security, I was directed to a hall-like room filled with numerous seats teeming with individuals waiting for their own interviews. As names were called one by one, guiding people to specific rooms, I observed some emerging from those rooms in tears or with sorrowful expressions. Some were even escorted out by security. Naturally, this heightened my apprehension, and I sought answers from a fellow interviewee seated beside me. They explained that those who appeared distraught or unhappy upon leaving the rooms had been denied a visa. This revelation only intensified my anxiety, and doubts crept into my mind, making it difficult to imagine being granted a visa. I mentally prepared myself for the worst outcome, accepting that rejection was a possibility.

Before my name was called, I decided to take a moment to compose myself. I entered the restroom and splashed water on my face, peering into the mirror. The outcome of this interview would be a life-changing moment, whether positive or negative. Although a visa denial wouldn't devastate me at that time, in that critical moment, prayer became my strongest weapon. In a soft voice, I uttered, "May your will be done, Lord. I trust in you."

Stepping out of the restroom, I was startled to hear my name being called, urging me to proceed to room 2. My hands trembled and my heart raced like a sprinter at full speed. My body seemed to have a mind of its own, shaking uncontrollably, but I summoned the strength to enter the room.

As I pushed open the door, I was greeted by an American lady seated on the other side of a glass partition. She initiated the conversation by asking how I was feeling, and I couldn't help but admit my nervousness. To my surprise, she reassured me and displayed unexpected warmth and friendliness. We chatted about various aspects of my life, and her genuine interest put me at ease, gradually soothing my trembling. Eventually, she inquired about my possessions, and I feared this would be the point of denial. Despite my concerns, I chose honesty and simply replied, "It's just me; I don't own anything."

After typing something on her computer, I anxiously awaited her response. Doubt crept in, and I silently called out to God, wondering where he was in that moment. Finally, she said those unforgettable words, "Derrick, your visa has been approved." Stunned, I struggled to comprehend her words, prompting her to repeat them. It took a moment for the realization to sink in, and I momentarily froze. Perceiving my delayed reaction, she handed me a receipt and jokingly suggested I leave before she changed her mind.

Thanking the kind lady as I exited the room, I inadvertently bumped my head against the door in my excitement. Laughter erupted from the people in the hallway, but I paid no attention. My mind was elsewhere, filled with disbelief and gratitude. Overflowing with joy, I silently praised God as I left the embassy.

Still in a state of disbelief, I approached someone who had just left the embassy and asked them about the indication of a successful visa application. They confirmed that a blue receipt was given to those whose visas were approved. I was on the verge of clapping my hands with joy. The person then inquired if I had received a ticket, and when I confirmed that I had, they expressed their happiness for me, acknowledging that I was blessed. Their words reminded me of the disappointment they must have faced with their own visa denial, evoking a tinge of sadness.

I made my way to the roadside in search of a taxi to the restaurant where Ferry eagerly awaited my return. Rain began to pour, but I paid no heed, standing there unaffected by the downpour. Fortunately, a motorcyclist offered me a ride to the restaurant. Along the journey, he was sociable and friendly. Upon learning of my approved visa, he shared my joy and wished me the best.

Ferry eagerly stood up upon spotting me. Initially wearing a somber expression to pretend I hadn't got it, I approached her, but as she hugged me tightly, I couldn't hold back my smile. In the midst of the restaurant, she let out a loud exclamation, capturing everyone's attention. Unfazed by the curious onlookers, she requested to see the visa, and I proudly presented the blue receipt. Together, we read the accompanying instructions, outlining when I should return to the embassy to collect my passport with the visa. Ferry wasted no time calling her parents, friends, and everyone in her contact list to share the exciting news. As for me, I glanced at my phone, overwhelmed by the desire to express my gratitude to someone, anyone, but unable to find the right words. The magnitude of what had transpired was still sinking in.

God had worked wonders in my life, and while others had spoken of his love for me, the events of that day brought tears of joy to my eyes. Some might dismiss it as just a visa, but I had prayed for opportunities to travel abroad since I was five years old in 2003. It took another fourteen years before I obtained my first overseas visa in 2017, and it was for a country known for its stringent vetting process and high visa denial rates, especially for individuals from third-world countries like Uganda. Many of those I knew who had been denied visas seemed more financially stable and had possessions I lacked. Their discouragement and labeling of the visa application as a waste of time and resources had initially affected me. Yet, it was during this journey that I witnessed the hand of God making a way and opening doors, for which I remain grateful to this day. I used to attribute it to luck, but upon reflection, I realized something extraordinary had guided me.

Once I got back home. I attempted to watch television, but my mind was still lost in disbelief. My roommate rejoiced on my behalf and suggested we celebrate—an invitation I readily accepted. Our celebration continued until late into the night. (To this day, those who know about my visa approval still wonder how it was possible without any special connections or undisclosed circumstances. I eventually gave up on trying to explain the unexplainable, opting instead to cherish the gift that had been bestowed upon me.)

The following morning, I awoke to find that Ferry had gone ahead and purchased our tickets to the United States, even sending me copies as proof. Tears welled up in my eyes, for in that moment, it became undeniably real. I would be embarking on my first-ever journey overseas.

During this time, I shared the incredible news of my visa approval and imminent visit to the United States with my cousin, who met with me ready to help with my visa application to the UK. He was taken aback, struggling to believe the extraordinary turn of events. After explaining the details, he offered his sincere congratulations and expressed genuine happiness for me. Without hesitation, he entrusted me with the documents, instructing me to keep them safe. He assured me that upon my return from the States, should I choose to pursue a visa for the United Kingdom, he would gladly lend his assistance.

~ 17 ~

Travel

On the long-awaited due date, both Ferry and I brimmed with excitement—Ferry, for having been away from her family for an extended period, and me, as a first-time visitor to the United States, regarding the momentous occasion of meeting her family. In the airport, as the hum of conversations and the hurried footsteps of fellow travelers filled the air, my thoughts started to wander. The daunting reality of being thousands of feet above the ground tugged at the edges of my consciousness, and my emotions swayed like a pendulum. With an inherent fear of heights lingering within me and a sense of unpreparedness for what lay ahead, I braced myself for the unknown, knowing that there was no turning back now.

As the boarding call echoed through the bustling terminal, we made our way onto the aircraft, the gateway to new horizons. Serendipity smiled upon me as Ferry had managed to secure me a coveted window seat, a vantage point I had long yearned for. The idea of witnessing the world from above, like a bird in flight, excited me. However, as the plane commenced its ascent, my initial joy morphed into a cocktail of trepidation and anxiety. With wide-eyed nervousness, I pressed my gaze against the window. The ground beneath us began to shrink, transforming familiar landscapes into intricate tapestries of color and shape from high above.

The grip of fear tightened its hold on me as the altitude increased, leaving me grappling with conflicting emotions. Clinging to my seat with all my strength, I sought solace in the rhythmic hum of the aircraft's engines. The vastness of the sky and the seemingly fragile wings that carried us through it triggered a profound sense of vulnerability within me. In an attempt to regain composure, I squeezed my eyes shut, blocking out the vertigo-inducing views that lay just beyond the window.

It was during this introspective moment that memories from my past came flooding back, like a movie reel playing in the depths of my mind. I was transported to a time when the idea of venturing beyond familiar shores was nothing more than a whimsical dream, whispered promises of a younger version of myself. Every time I gazed at the sky, transfixed by the sight of airplanes gracefully soaring above me, a deep-rooted desire would stir within my heart. In those fleeting moments, I couldn't help but imagine myself aboard one of those planes, embarking on an extraordinary journey to a distant land. I would silently utter a prayer, "Oh God, may the day come when I find myself on that very plane, traversing the skies and exploring the wonders of far-off lands."

In the midst of my swirling emotions, I gradually opened my eyes, allowing reality to seep in. The aircraft had reached a stable altitude, and the once-tumultuous ascent had given way to a serene cruising altitude. The turbulence within me settled, replaced by a sense of awe and wonder at the vast expanse beside me and excitement at the playing out of a long-held dream. Gratitude overflowed within me, and I offered heartfelt thanks to the Lord for his boundless goodness and enduring love. This inaugural flight, apart from the initial ascent, was proving to be less daunting than anticipated.

Nearly twenty-four hours later, we touched down at LAX airport for a stopover, and I was exhausted, having had each instance of turbulence jolt me awake in the terror that something might be amiss with the aircraft. The lengthy queues at Immigration only compounded my weariness, but once the other formalities concluded, we emerged from the airport into the United States of America.

I immediately sensed a difference in the air I breathed. The aroma was distinct, like a different type of oxygen. Breathing through my mouth, unable to tolerate the unfamiliar atmosphere with my nostrils alone, I initially attributed the sensation to airport fumes. However, I soon realized it pervaded wherever I ventured. It took me nearly two weeks to acclimate to this unfamiliar air.

The Christmas season in LA was in full swing, and winter had descended upon the city—an unfamiliar experience for me as I come from a tropical climate, where such cold weather is unheard of. The icy temperatures took me by surprise, causing my ears to pop and leaving me bewildered about the sensations my body was experiencing. During our brief sojourn in Los Angeles, I marveled at its vibrant surroundings, harboring a desire to dwell in a similar metropolis adorned with the towering skyscrapers of my childhood dreams. I even offered a brief prayer to God, expressing my willingness to reside in a city akin to LA if it aligned with his divine plan.

Upon evening's arrival, we returned to the airport, encountering an older gentleman in the check-in line. He struggled to scan my passport, prompting him to scrutinize its origin. Upon realizing it hailed from Uganda, he quipped, "It's been a while since I last saw one of these. How is Idi Amin?" Astonished, I burst into laughter, realizing that his knowledge of my country seemed limited to the infamous Amin. Our ensuing conversation allowed me to shed light on Uganda, albeit without delving deep into the details of Amin's demise, known to me only as an exiled ruler.

Stepping off the final plane in San Francisco after three grueling days of travel, jet lag firmly gripped my senses, but we still needed to get to Ferry's house. Ferry's father, Robert, stood poised at Arrivals to welcome us. As it marked our initial meeting, I chose to greet him with a bashful smile before assuming a reserved demeanor. To shield us from the biting cold, Robert thoughtfully presented us with a couple of jackets. Unaccustomed to such attire, I initially questioned the necessity of wearing one. However, I soon discovered the error of my ways. The second I alighted from the vehicle, after napping the entire ride, I was immediately assailed by an unprecedented chill. The sensation mirrored that of stepping into a refrigerator, intensified by my tropical origins. Shivering uncontrollably, I yearned for the warmth of the indoors and eagerly hurried inside, clutching suitcases as I sought refuge.

Once ensconced in our heated but temporary abode, the mere thought of venturing outdoors evoked aversion. Nevertheless, the enticing prospect of satiating my hunger beckoned. Despite the numbing cold, Ferry and her father insisted we venture out to a local restaurant. Although I was enthusiastic upon encountering the delightful aroma of food, I found myself perusing a menu that appeared entirely foreign to me, save for the sight of fries and a burger—a glimmer of something familiar amid the bewildering choices. Though tempted to seek guidance from Ferry and Robert, my pride hindered me from doing so. Consequently, I settled on ordering a burger and fries. As I waited for my meal to arrive, I glanced out the frost-encrusted windows, marveling at the unbelievable spectacle before me. I was clad in a jacket and sporting my trusty Converse, but my feet began to feel like they were freezing. When our food was finally served, I struggled to steady my trembling hands, a consequence of the bone-chilling cold. To my surprise, Ferry and Robert remained unaffected, seemingly impervious to the wintry conditions. Returning to the hotel, I eagerly slipped beneath the covers, experiencing a blissful night of sleep akin to that of a contented infant.

The next day, we visited the school where Ferry had previously taught, and warm greetings were exchanged with her former colleagues and the children. Then I was given a guided tour of San Francisco's iconic landmarks. Finally, I beheld with my own eyes the sights that had long captivated me through cinematic portrayals—the majestic Golden Gate Bridge. I also stepped into the vastness of the ocean for the very first time, marveling at its beauty despite its chilling embrace, then hastening my retreat from its icy clutches.

As evening descended, we embarked on a northward drive to Lincoln, the abode of Robert's family. There, I was greeted by two fluffy felines, initially described as shy creatures. To my surprise, they gravitated toward me with astonishing speed, settling comfortably beside me on the couch. Perchance, I had become the first cocoa-hued gentleman they had encountered, leaving them perplexed and intrigued by this novel addition to their world. We then ventured out for dinner on our inaugural evening. Aware of my affinity for fish, Ferry sought to introduce me to one of her favorite cuisines—sushi. All eyes at the table fixated on me, curious to witness my first encounter with this exotic delicacy. Sadly, I took my first bite, only to be overwhelmed by an indescribable sense of disgust. Deciding to give it another chance, I took a second bite, but my stomach vehemently rebelled. Without warning, I bolted toward the restroom, my body convulsing as I uncontrollably emptied the contents of my stomach. The scene left everyone around me concerned and sympathetic. Robert kindly inquired if there was an alternative I could consume, but regrettably, I couldn't bring myself to try anything else.

Upon my recovery the following day, we embarked on a road trip to Arizona to meet the extended family, a gathering Ferry was determined not to miss. It was an opportunity for me to meet relatives I had yet to acquaint myself with, as I had only known a few of them. This marked my first road trip within the United States, and it seemed that every mile we traversed invited me to surrender to slumber's embrace as I was still jet lagged. However, as we ascended, my ears popped repeatedly. Sharing my discomfort with the others, Robert deduced it was likely due to the altitude. He offered me a piece of chewing gum, which miraculously alleviated the discomfort. It became apparent that my ears were unaccustomed to the high altitude and cold weather, subjecting me to this sensation. Meeting with Robert's father and family was to be a surprise, and witnessing the arrival of his granddaughter elicited wonder and filled the room with joy and warmth.

During our time in Arizona, we explored the sights, although my ongoing struggle with food persisted. Every new culinary experience left me feeling unfamiliar and hesitant, until I stumbled upon the reliable comfort of burgers, a favorite that sustained me throughout the trip. We strolled through Scottsdale, and my eyes beheld the spectacle of supercars for the first time. Overflowing with excitement, I snapped numerous pictures as proof, eager to share my adventures with friends back home.

Once back in Lincoln, Ferry's family welcomed several families into the home to celebrate and revel in the holiday spirit. Curiosity surrounded my presence, and I willingly shared stories of my origins, relishing the opportunity to educate and engage with those eager to learn. Ferry's family embraced me warmly, their inquisitive nature a testament to their affection and concern for their daughter. Despite our shared struggles with initiating conversations, Ferry's father and I found common ground, forging a connection that transcended words and allowed for meaningful interactions and shared moments of enjoyment.

With only a week remaining before my departure, I managed to reconnect with American friends I had met during previous mission trips. Additionally, I longed to revisit the church I had dedicated years of service to. We decided to attend a Sunday church service at *Bridgeway Christian Church*, eagerly preparing ourselves for the spiritual gathering.

Stepping into the church, I was greeted by surprised friends who hadn't expected to see me on American soil. The joy of being in a church I had heard so much about overwhelmed me, reminding me of the wondrous ways God orchestrates our paths. Although the expected pastor was absent, Pastor Brian Kiley delivered a sermon on relationships and marriages that resonated deeply within me. His words penetrated my heart, leaving a lasting impact and inspiring transformative decisions. After the service, I savored conversations with friends.

The cold weather made outdoor excursions challenging, but despite it, Robert, Ferry, and their family made definite plans to ensure that I didn't leave the States without a snow experience. Their enthusiasm was contagious, and I gladly accepted their offer to take me to see the snow. They made sure I was well-prepared for the cold, providing me with all the layers of clothing they could find to protect me from the freezing temperatures. Excitement filled the air as we embarked on a journey up the mountains to Donner Park. When we arrived, I couldn't contain my joy and excitement; I was all smiles and eager to dive into the snow. They had to remind me to be careful because all I wanted to do was run to the snow. And there, amid the serene beauty of the snowcapped landscape, I had my very first encounter with snow. It was like a dream come true, something I had previously only seen in movies, but now it was within my reach, and I reveled

144

in the magical experience of seeing and touching snow for the very first time.

The warmth of their hospitality and the unforgettable snow experience created cherished memories that will stay with me forever. Throughout my journey, I had many new experiences—culinary, climatic, linguistic, and cultural. These were aspects I hadn't fully thought of while dreaming of travel, yet I remained grateful for the opportunity to immerse myself in American life and appreciate the organized nature of the country compared to my homeland.

Time seemed to slip away, and with just a few days left, we made the most of our remaining time, visiting places and allowing Ferry to reconnect with her friends. I even experienced the peculiar sensation of driving on the opposite side of the road, a stark difference from the norms in my native Uganda.

On our final day, we attended a movie screening after bidding farewell to friends at a memorable house party. Interacting with young people my age, I relished the conversations and connections forged before we ventured to the cinema. As the day drew to a close, we packed our suitcases, and accompanied by a longtime mutual friend, we made our way to the airport. Sitting on the plane, I buckled up for the long flight home, contemplating what the future held for us upon our return. Our upcoming trip to Rwanda danced on the horizon, and while a part of me wished to stay in the States a little longer, duty beckoned us homeward.

When we boarded the plane at San Francisco airport and settled in for the journey, thoughts swirled in my mind. I couldn't help but wonder what awaited us upon our return. With a single day's respite at home, we would embark on yet another adventure, traveling to Rwanda, guided by the knowledge that our time in the States had left an indelible mark on our hearts and minds.

The flight to Rwanda was brief, but upon arrival, I was rendered mute by the breathtaking sights that unfolded before me. Rwanda, a small and enchanting country, greeted us with its pristine lakes and majestic mountains that stirred my soul. The meticulous cleanliness and remarkable organization of Rwanda left a lasting impression, and I found myself wholeheartedly drawn to its charm and beauty.

During our stay in Rwanda, we explored its vibrant capital city, Kigali. Nestled in the heart of the nation, Kigali boasts rolling hills, valleys, and ridges connected by steep slopes. We visited significant memorial sites, including the Kigali Genocide Memorial, and gained a deeper understanding of the resilience and strength of its people. We also ventured into the mountains, exploring breathtaking locations that Ferry's friends had recommended, as well as enjoying the serene beauty of a picturesque beach.

Although we encountered language barriers due to the four languages spoken there, our communication struggles dissolved when we encountered someone fluent in English. It was a relief to finally manage to connect with locals and navigate our way through the rich picture of Rwandan culture. Interestingly, many people we encountered initially mistook me for a Rwandan, leading them to try and talk to me in their native tongue. Confusion prevailed as I couldn't comprehend their words, often resorting to presenting my passport as proof of my foreign identity. Nonetheless, these encounters allowed me to glimpse the warmth and hospitality of the Rwandan people.

A visit to a tattoo shop was a memorable experience. Ferry tried to persuade me to join her in getting a tattoo, but my aversion to needles and low pain tolerance compelled me to resist. However, a pivotal moment arrived when I witnessed Ferry shed a tear during her own tattoo session, prompting me to firmly decline the offer, realizing the wisdom of my decision.

On our final day in Rwanda, I had the joyous opportunity of meeting one of my Rwandan friends, whom I had only interacted with online. We spent a delightful day together, exploring the vibrant streets of Kigali before capping off our time with a movie and a shared dinner.

Reflecting on our time in the United States and Rwanda, Ferry and I had navigated through numerous moments that revealed the stark differences between us. It became evident that pursuing a romantic relationship was not the path we were meant to take. After carefully considering our compatibility, I made the heartfelt decision to remain friends, recognizing the value of our connection in a different capacity.

Although Ferry initially distanced herself upon hearing my decision, our bond eventually grew stronger as we reestablished our friendship.

~ 18 ~

Back Home

Back home, I eagerly shared the tales of my two journeys. The sheer joy of indulging in the diverse range of cuisines I had missed, relishing each mouthwatering delicacy at my whim, was simply sublime. Gone were the days of lugging around a jacket everywhere I went, and I reveled in the pleasure of basking in the rejuvenating embrace of fresh, invigorating air once more.

Yet, amid the excitement of being home, my heart yearned for more. My sojourns to the United States and Rwanda had unsettled me, clouding my perception of home. While I resumed my normal routine, the mundaneness of it all paled. Only the passion I held for soccer provided a spark of excitement. Conversations with my roommate inevitably gravitated toward my experiences in the States, and I found myself vividly describing the sensation of life within a refrigerator, a realm of bone-chilling coldness that exceeded my wildest imaginations. Every recollection I shared seemed to blow his mind, just as it had blown mine.

Alas, the comforting embrace of my familiar Ugandan existence eluded me. I found myself on bended knees, beseeching divine intervention to open doors that would transport me elsewhere. In the depths of my longing, the offer extended by my cousin resurfaced in my thoughts, prompting me to reach out and inquire about his willingness to assist me. Though preoccupied at the time, he assured me that we could embark on this journey together in a month's time.

During the intervening period, I exercised patience, diligently setting aside funds earned from my labor for the opportune moment when their necessity would be paramount. It was then that fate intervened, as one of my colleagues introduced me to his brother from the Netherlands, who happened to be visiting Uganda for a week. Bound by our shared love for soccer, we quickly forged a friendship, and he extended an invitation to visit him upon his return home, offering the prospect of securing a spot on a team in Amsterdam.

With seemingly miraculous swiftness, visas were acquired and, while reluctant to forsake the arrangement with my cousin's brother, I resolved to seize the chance to explore the Netherlands since I possessed the coveted travel document. Thus, the following week saw me boarding a plane to Amsterdam to join my newfound companion. However, fate dealt an unexpected blow, as the team he had intended to connect me with was embroiled in a financial crisis, rendering their ability to recruit me impossible, despite their admiration for the skills I displayed during training. Faced with this setback, I embarked on a quest to find an alternative team, tirelessly searching each day for a new opportunity.

Amsterdam, for all its charm, revealed itself to be a realm foreign to my spirit. Every passing day brought with it an inexplicable sense of soul-draining melancholy, as if the very essence of my being were being sapped by the surroundings. In light of this realization, I made the decision to bid farewell to my pursuit of a soccer team and return home. Within a mere week, I found myself back home, where a bittersweet contentment washed over me, grateful for the experiences gained but no longer eager to venture back.

Back in Uganda, I clung to hope, fervently praying for my cousin's brother to come through for me. Life in my homeland had lost its luster, leaving me feeling isolated despite the presence of my roommate. After much deliberation, my cousin's brother consulted an immigration lawyer. When his demands for financial compensation loomed before us, we resolved to pool our resources, working tirelessly to amass the required funds before proceeding to the next steps. Yet, this proved to be a formidable challenge, prompting me to explore the possibility of securing an additional job to bolster my savings.

In the span of a few weeks, I fortuitously crossed paths with my friend Boy, who was involved with an organization dedicated to assisting orphaned children in their educational pursuits. Boy, aware of my amateur photography skills, approached me with an intriguing opportunity. They needed a photographer for an upcoming weekend event, and he wondered if I would be available to lend him my talents. While photography had been a mere hobby for me thus far, the prospect of being compensated for my work immediately sparked my interest.

When the weekend arrived, I accompanied Boy to the organization's venue, only to discover that a sports event was taking place—a realization that initially unnerved me. Doubts crept into my mind, questioning whether my photographs would meet their standards. Nevertheless, I embarked on the task, capturing moments from midday until evening. Immersed in the spirited atmosphere of a soccer competition, a game dear to my heart, I found myself thoroughly enjoying the experience. Thankfully, I was not burdened with the responsibility of editing the images. I promptly returned the camera, receiving payment for my services before heading home and eagerly awaited the verdict.

To my delight and surprise, the organization expressed their satisfaction with my photographs, showcasing them on their website. They extended their gratitude to Boy for introducing them to a young, talented photographer—a compliment that blessed me, despite not considering myself a professional at the time.

During the sports event, Boy divulged his involvement in the real estate industry, sharing that it was a lucrative venture. Given my financial needs, I decided to give it a try, intrigued by the prospect of working alongside my friends while exploring various locations. It felt more like spending time together rather than laboring at a particular place. Consequently, I bid farewell to my previous job selling refurbished computers and began a full-time role as a broker assistant in the real estate business.

A New Connection

Our work demanded constant movement, an aspect I thoroughly relished as it allowed me to encounter towns and cities I had never before set foot in. While this endeavor enabled me to save some money, it remained insufficient to cover the expenses associated with the visa process. Faced with this problem, I confided in Boy, sharing my predicament and the intricacies of the visa application. He questioned why I hadn't considered returning to the United States, where I had some friends. However, those connections, while present, did not possess the depth of understanding or the support system I longed for during challenging times.

Nonetheless, Boy revealed that he knew someone he trusted in the United States who could potentially help and be there for me when needed. This revelation filled me with hope, although the person's identity remained a mystery. I sought guidance through prayer, consulting with my cousin about this newfound possibility. Initially hesitant, as he wished for me to join him, my cousin eventually recognized the practicality of returning to the States, given the uncertainty surrounding the UK visa process.

The following day, I approached Boy once again, requesting him to contact the person he had mentioned. Despite our attempts to reach out while in each other's company, the individual did not answer. However, Boy assured me that he would establish contact and relay their response in a few days.

After a week of anticipation, Boy received a response from Ivan, Astonishingly, he welcomed me to the United States. Ivan provided his contact number, encouraging direct communication to facilitate our future plans. That evening, I reached out to him via a mobile app, and the conversation gradually alleviated my initial apprehensions. The more we spoke, the more at ease I felt in his presence.

Ivan inquired about my intended travel dates to the States, to which I responded with "very soon," despite still needing to gather the remaining funds for my airfare. I informed him of my plan to finalize everything within a month, and he expressed his agreement, requesting that I inform him when I was ready. Having already saved half of the required amount for the ticket, I took precautions by keeping the funds separate, mindful of the possibility of using them for other expenses if they remained within easy reach.

Broken Trust
and the Option

uring that challenging period, my unwavering trust was placed in my friend Boy. Recognizing the importance of safeguarding the money I had saved, I made the decision to entrust it to someone close to me, and Boy was the only viable option at that time. I approached him and discussed the matter, and he graciously agreed to hold onto the money for me.

I handed over the amount to Boy, with clear instructions to keep it safe and only return it to me once I had gathered the remaining funds necessary to purchase an air ticket. My trust in Boy was unwavering, and I felt that my life depended on this money. While it could have been tempting to have it in my possession, I believed that keeping it with Boy was a wise choice.

As I relentlessly pursued ways to raise the remaining funds as quickly as possible, I took on various side jobs in addition to my real estate role. However, my efforts seemed insufficient, and I found myself growing weary and disheartened. One night, after reading my Bible and feeling exhausted, I sought solace through prayer, asking God for open doors and guidance. As I prayed, my phone began to ring, causing a momentary distraction. Determined to maintain my focus, I ended my prayer abruptly to silence the phone.

It was my cousin calling—an unusual occurrence at such a late hour, considering he knew it was nighttime. I shared my concerns and the stress I was experiencing regarding the funds for my air ticket. My cousin sympathized with my situation and asked about the amount I needed to raise. After discussing it in detail, he unexpectedly offered to provide me with the money he had raised for the visa processing. I was overwhelmed with gratitude and could hardly believe his generosity. I gladly accepted his kind offer, and he promptly sent me the funds before I retired to bed that night. Overwhelmed with relief, I offered heartfelt thanks to the Lord for his love and provision, and I drifted off to sleep, knowing that my journey to the United States was within reach.

The following morning, as soon as I woke up, I immediately contacted Ivan. Although I was unable to reach him directly, I left a message informing him that I was prepared and ready for the trip. I had gathered everything I needed and was eager to proceed. I went to work that day, eagerly awaiting the moment I could inform Boy about the positive turn of events. When I saw him, I couldn't contain my excitement, and I joyfully shared the news that I had secured the remaining funds. Boy was genuinely happy for me and inquired about my intended departure date, to which I replied that I hadn't finalized it yet.

After completing my work for the day, I called Ivan. Together, we planned and agreed on a departure date that was set for a month later, shortly after the Easter season. The next step was to purchase my plane ticket, and I intended to do so the following day. I promptly messaged Boy, informing him that I would collect the money he had been keeping for me so that I could proceed with buying the air ticket.

Normally, Boy would respond promptly to my messages, but that night he remained unresponsive, leading me to believe he was asleep. Not wanting to disturb him, I decided to give him a call the next morning, giving him advance notice before our meeting later in the day. However, his reply came in the form of a brief "okay" text, which was uncharacteristic of him. Nevertheless, I brushed it off, assuming he might be having a difficult day.

At work, when I saw Boy, he inquired about my departure plans, and I shared my intention to go together after work so he could withdraw the money and provide it to me in cash. But when evening came, Boy was nowhere to be found. He ignored my calls, leaving me increasingly frustrated. Trying to contain my anger and disappointment, I sent him a text, requesting him to call me once he received my message. Boy's response finally arrived close to midnight. His message stated that he had been caught up with something and had left work early, promising to give me the money the following day. Although I was angry, I chose to trust him and patiently waited for the next day. Being open with my emotions, I asked him to be honest with me rather than leave me in suspense, but Boy continued to present excuses, ultimately failing to provide me with the money. It was at this point that I began to believe that he had no intention of returning my money and that he had deceived me. Boy had been one of the few individuals I'd placed my utmost trust in, and his betrayal shattered my heart. I felt a surge of panic and helplessness, not knowing what to do next. Without any backup plan in place, I saw my future crumbling in the hands of the person I had trusted the most.

Seeking solace, I turned to prayer, pouring out my heart and shedding tears as a means of releasing the pain and confusion within me. I lost my appetite, withdrawing from conversations with others. The subsequent day, Boy failed to show up at work, and my attempts to contact him through calls and texts went unanswered. It was the final blow, and I considered involving the police. However, I hesitated, not wanting to see someone I had shared a significant portion of my life with being incarcerated. I felt utterly helpless. The stress and depression caused me to lose even more weight, exacerbating my already thin frame.

Accepting the fact that I would not recover the lost money, I found myself losing trust in Ivan too, partly because I had come to know him through Boy, leaving me torn as to who to confide in. However, Ivan's straightforward demeanor did seem somewhat trustworthy, especially given his maturity. Despite my reservations, circumstances left me with no alternative but to rely on him, as he became my only option at that critical juncture. I reached out to Ivan to inform him of the changes in my plans. I admitted that the dates for my departure would be delayed. I began to contemplate ways to secure funds as quickly as possible, though I was afraid to confide in others about what had transpired. After days of deep introspection, I realized that I had to find a solution rapidly if I was to realize my dream of flying to the United States.

Though I still didn't have an answer regarding the fate of my lost money, one thing became clear—I had to rely on divine intervention and seek a miracle.

A Conversation Overheard

Days passed, and the weight of my circumstances bore down heavily on me; however, there was one place where I could escape it all and find a fleeting sense of peace—the soccer field. Surrounded by friends while chasing after a ball, and our friendly competing, I could momentarily forget about my troubles. It was on one of these days, as the game concluded, that I happened to overhear my fellow players engrossed in a conversation about their aspirations of starting a business. They discussed the possibility of borrowing money to make their dreams a reality. Their words planted a seed of curiosity and hope. Could I, too, find a way to secure a loan and bridge the remaining gap in my finances to purchase that crucial air ticket?

From that moment on, the idea consumed my thoughts. I pondered the feasibility of seeking a loan without any collateral, knowing that it would be an uphill battle. I set out to compile a list of potential lenders who might be willing to trust me without imposing such stringent requirements. Trust, I realized, would be the key factor in convincing someone to take a chance on me. Starting from the top of my list, I embarked on a series of conversations, presenting my case and laying bare my hopes and dreams. Each rejection was a blow, a checkmark against my hopefulness. Days turned into weeks as I tirelessly pursued this elusive goal, never losing sight of my objective. I reached out to friends and acquaintances, exploring every possible avenue for assistance.

It was during this exhaustive process that I approached my cousin's girlfriend, a close friend I had established a deep and long-standing connection with. While hesitant at first, she possessed the necessary funds to potentially help me. I saw this as my golden opportunity, a glimmer of hope in an otherwise dim landscape. With all my persuasive skills at the ready, I outlined my repayment plan, emphasizing my commitment and the specific amount I needed, although deep down, I was uncertain about how I would fulfill my promises.

160

She requested time for consideration, and during that anxious waiting period, I sought divine intervention to touch her heart. As fate would have it, I frequently encountered Boy at work, our interactions brief and strained. His presence served as a constant reminder of his betrayal. But in his unfailing mercy, God answered my prayers. My cousin's girlfriend wanted to meet at a designated bank to withdraw and provide me with the money. The hours at work that day dragged on, every tick of the clock an eternity, until I finally found myself standing outside the bank, my heart pounding.

When I left the bank with the funds securely in my possession, I struggled to contain my emotions. Tears of happiness streamed down my face, mingling with a sense of disbelief. A burden had been lifted from my shoulders, and a path had finally opened up before me. The impossible was now within reach. Without a moment's hesitation, I rushed to purchase my air ticket, savoring the sweet taste of victory. Later that night, I called Ivan, my voice brimming with excitement, and I informed him that I was ready to fly over. I specified the dates stated on my air ticket, alleviating any concerns he might have had. The air ticket, the final piece of the puzzle, was now secured.

Returning home after acquiring the ticket, I shared the news with my roommate, the mix of emotions that accompanied this revelation palpable—a heady blend of relief, elation, and trepidation. The countdown to my departure had officially begun. In the following days, I threw myself into preparations, meticulously packing the belongings I deemed necessary for this new chapter of my life. Ivan had also requested specific items, and I made sure to include them in my suitcase. With each folded shirt and zipped-up bag, the reality of my impending journey grew more tangible.

As the departure date loomed closer, a sense of nervousness settled deep within me of the profound impact this move would have on my life. Caught between embracing and fearing these impending shifts, I bid farewell to most of my close friends and some family members. The weight of their goodbyes, tinged with apprehension and hope, lingered in the air. But despite the uncertainties that lay ahead, I clung to a sense of optimism. I placed my faith in God, trusting that whatever awaited me on the other side of the world would lead me down a path of growth and fulfillment. And with that, I took a deep breath, ready to embark on this extraordinary journey.

– *20* –

The Journey

I n the days leading up to my long-awaited departure, a sense of weakness began to pervade my body. Initially, I attributed it to the natural nervousness that accompanies such a significant life transition. However, as the final day drew near, an unrelenting dizziness and a soaring fever seized hold of me, leaving me deeply concerned about my well-being. Undeterred, I sought immediate medical attention, hoping for a swift resolution. To my dismay, the diagnosis I received was far from what I had expected. The doctor's words landed upon me like a thunderbolt: malaria. The revelation struck me with an overwhelming mix of shock and anxiety. Time was not on my side, as I had insufficient days to fully recover before my scheduled departure. Desperation gripped my heart.

Summoning all my courage, I implored the doctor to prescribe the most potent and expedient treatment available, driven by an intense desire to regain my health as quickly as possible. However, this course of action came with an unexpected cost. Reluctantly, I made the difficult decision to dip into the savings I had diligently set aside for my journey, knowing that it was a necessary sacrifice to ensure my recovery and the realization of my dreams.

With my flight scheduled for the following day and a three-day prescription in my possession, a new thought presented itself. Carrying medication on an international flight without the requisite documentation was a daunting prospect. In a bid to overcome this hurdle, I cautiously concealed a few tablets within the confines of my pockets. I was also worried about how to discreetly administer the medication during the flight. The prospect of managing this delicate task while adhering to the strict regulations and watchful eyes of airport security and airline staff was nerve-racking.

On the day of my departure from my homeland, despite feeling feverish, dizzy, and barely able to stand, I pushed myself to the limit. Early in the morning, I expressed heartfelt gratitude to my roommate, who had been a pillar of support and resembled a brother during my time of need. Although weak, I managed to bid farewell to the family I had grown up with.

My roommate kindly accompanied me to the airport in a taxi. Along the way, I gazed out of the car window, absorbing the sights of everything I was leaving behind. Uncertain of when or how I would return, I entrusted myself to God's hands. He had been my unwavering source of support throughout my life.

I arrived several hours ahead of schedule. Concerned for my well-being, my roommate offered to wait with me, but I assured him that I would manage on my own. I had four more hours to kill, but I rested and waited patiently for check-in, where I determinedly navigated through the scrutiny of document checks to receive and proceed to Immigration, where a similar process ensued. Weary from the repetitive scrutiny, I couldn't help but question why I had chosen to shave my beard and hair, inadvertently making myself appear even younger than my actual age.

Taking my seat at the boarding gate, I began talking with a cleaner who worked at the airport. Like others before him, he, too, wondered about my age and travel arrangements. Boarding commenced, and as I passed through the scanning area, I realized I still had Ugandan shillings in my pocket that I could not use in my destination. My intuition led me to give all the money to the cleaner I had met earlier. In return, he offered a heartfelt prayer, filling me with a sense of happiness and peace. With that, I boarded the plane, ready to embark on my journey.

As the aircraft took off, I gazed out the window, engulfed in a whirlwind of emotions. Thoughts of what I had left behind mingled with apprehension about the unknown that awaited me. Yet, in the depths of my being, I held steadfast trust in God, praying that this venture was aligned with His will.

During the flight, I diligently followed my medication regimen, but the timing became uncertain during a layover in Amsterdam. Without access to my suitcase, which contained the rest of my medication, I persevered through the discomfort of shivering and a high fever. Eventually, I boarded another plane, bound for Los Angeles. I struggled to sleep so my body could heal faster, but I couldn't, and my appetite was nonexistent, causing me to skip the meals offered onboard.

Upon landing at the Los Angeles airport, my need to retrieve my medication grew. However, I faced another hurdle: passing through Immigration before accessing my bags. To my surprise, the Immigration line was unusually long, intensifying my concerns about potential complications or even denial of entry. Entrusting my fate to prayer, I gathered my strength and endured the wait, all the while feeling increasingly dizzy. To my relief, the immigration process went smoother than expected, with only a few routine questions. A smile of gratitude crept onto my face, despite my overall weakened state. After successfully passing through Immigration, relief filled me when I was finally reunited with my bags, where I quickly retrieved my medication and took a moment to rest and compose myself. Ivan, who had graciously offered to pick me up from the airport, reassured me he was in the vicinity, which brought a renewed smile to my face.

As I kept going, I encountered a security guard who inquired about my solo travel. Presenting my passport, the guard commented on my youthful appearance. I couldn't help but acknowledge the repetitiveness of the situation, as it was the fifth time my age had been questioned. Approaching customs, I carried two suitcases—one filled with my personal belongings and the other predominantly containing items requested by Ivan. Unfortunately, one of the suitcases was flagged for additional inspection due to its contents. Given that it contained foodstuffs, namely Ugandan porridge, I understood the reason for the flagging and remained relatively unfazed. I trusted that the authorities would inspect the food and allow me to proceed.

To my surprise, I was escorted to a separate room, and before I could notify Ivan of the situation, my phone was confiscated, instantly alerting me to the gravity of the circumstances. An overwhelming sense of nervousness consumed me as I settled into a seat, anxiously awaiting the impending discussion. Three airport security guards entered the room, each taking part in the thorough examination of my suitcase. The suspicion arose from the fact that I had brought five kilograms of powdered Ugandan porridge, which inadvertently raised concerns about potential drug smuggling. Fear coursed through my veins.

Weary and unwell, I couldn't help but worry about the possibility of contamination in the testing equipment, which could yield a false positive for drugs. What would I do if that was to happen? The security guards meticulously subjected the porridge to multiple tests and bombarded me with questions about its composition. Despite my trembling state, I lacked detailed knowledge about the porridge's ingredients, as growing up, I had never paid much attention to its preparation. The entire ordeal extended for over two hours, further amplifying my anxiety.

It seemed every available drug expert at the airport was summoned to verify that the porridge was indeed not drugs. Fatigue began to set in for some of the security guards, but one of them tenaciously persisted in his efforts. He tirelessly conducted test after test until even he gave up. Eventually, I was cleared of any wrongdoing, but I had reached a point where, if given the choice, I would have willingly abandoned the porridge and moved on. My phone was returned to me, and I hurried to the airport exit. It was only then that I realized I needed to inform Ivan of my situation. Frustratingly, I discovered that I had no Wi-Fi access outside the airport, and I lacked a local cell phone number to make a call. Given all I had endured within the airport premises, I had no desire to reenter.

Desperate for a solution, I scrolled through the last messages Ivan had sent me, discovering that he had waited until he grew tired and left. His final message provided instructions for boarding a bus to a specific stop, where he would pick me up. Though I had no experience navigating buses in the United States, I possessed enough cash to cover the fare for the hour-long journey.

Upon arrival at the bus station near Ivan's house, I discovered that entry required an electronic payment method, which I lacked. Stranded with my suitcases, an observant employee noticed my predicament and kindly opened the electronic gates, allowing me to enter. Once again, my phone refused to establish a Wi-Fi connection, so I swallowed my nervousness and asked a fellow traveler if they could help me contact Ivan. To Ivan's disbelief, I had managed to traverse from the airport to the bus stop unaccompanied.

I remained at the bus stop for approximately two more hours until Ivan arrived and whisked me away in his car. Once I was sitting in his vehicle, I finally exhaled deeply. My arduous three-day journey from Uganda had come to an end. Exhausted and famished, I could hardly recall the last time I had eaten a proper meal. Despite my weakened state and persistent fever, I chose not to burden anyone with the knowledge of my illness, fearing embarrassment. Ivan kindly took me to a restaurant for dinner, yet even after everything I had endured, my appetite remained nonexistent. Nevertheless, I forced myself to take a few bites.

Ivan then graciously chauffeured me to his residence. The idea of finally indulging in some much-needed sleep was palpable, considering the relentless exhaustion that had plagued me throughout the preceding days, starting from the moment I'd stepped foot on my initial flight.

– 21 –

The Immigrant

*I*n the following weeks, I began my status as an immigrant, a story unfolding within the vibrant embrace of Los Angeles—the illustrious city that never sleeps. The ceaseless pulse of the metropolis, aglow in lights both day and night, stirred an unparalleled excitement in this young Ugandan boy. Coming here seemed like a dream come true, as if surely this extraordinary place would surpass all my expectations. Yet, unbeknownst to me, a tumultuous path lay ahead.

My search commenced for a spiritual haven that would harmonize with the cadence of my beliefs. As fate would have it, I stumbled upon a welcoming congregation, nestled conveniently close to my new abode. Stepping through the threshold of this sacred space, little did I anticipate the profound role it would play in shaping the trajectory of my new journey. Beyond its physical confines, this place revealed itself as an oasis of unity and belonging, woven together by a vibrant thread of diverse souls.

Amid the embrace of fellowship, I found myself crossing paths with kindred spirits, each extending a hand of friendship and sharing prayers that seemed to echo the very desires of my heart. These newfound connections transcended mere companionship; they became pillars of strength during the tumultuous seas of acclimatizing to a novel urban landscape. Intriguingly, I formed a special bond with the church pastors themselves, who expressed genuine interest in my narrative, often seeking to delve deeper into my story. Remarkably, one of the pastors had once trod the path of being a missionary in Africa, affording us a unique connection that fostered a profound understanding between us.

The young adult pastors were a vibrant couple whose warmth radiated like a beacon. Their open arms extended beyond the confines of the church's walls, welcoming me not just into the folds of the young adults' group, but also into their very home. In their guidance and genuine care, I discovered a seamless integration into church life, fostering a sense of unity and common purpose.

Richard

Amid the tapestry of connections, one particular thread gleamed with an especially brilliant hue—a friend called Richard, who swiftly evolved from an acquaintance into an invaluable companion. As a boxer, Richard embodied a remarkable athleticism. His calm and composed demeanor exuded a sense of tranquility that instantly put those around him at ease. With an approachable and friendly nature, he emanated an aura of genuine warmth, drawing people into his orbit with an inherent magnetism.

What truly set Richard apart was his profound and unwavering devotion to Christ Jesus. His heart overflowed with a profound love for his faith, which manifested itself in his constant quest for spiritual growth. His commitment to nurturing his relationship with God was a torch of inspiration for all who had the privilege of knowing him. And through it all, he maintained an infectious smile that seemed to radiate his inner joy and peace.

Physically, Richard stood at an average height, his unassuming stature serving as a canvas for the extraordinary personality that he carried. His presence was a testament to the power of humility and authenticity, and his dedication to both his physical pursuits and his spiritual journey left an indelible mark on those fortunate enough to walk alongside him.

What were once weekends shrouded in the anonymity of the cityscape morphed into moments of shared laughter, profound discourse, and spirited escapades. Our shared endeavors ranged from exploring the local cinema houses to taking leisurely strolls, to participating in spirited rounds of video games. Even the afterglow of a fulfilling church service became an opportunity to find solace in each other's presence, etching a sense of camaraderie and belonging deep within.

City Life

This chapter of my Los Angeles odyssey stands as a living testament to the potency of community and friendship. Beyond the notion of a place of worship, the doors of that church ushered me into a sanctuary of connections that would become lifelines of encouragement, empathy, and mutual growth. Amid the ceaseless ebb and flow of the city's dynamic energy, these relationships remained steadfast anchors, grounding me in a haven of shared spirituality and kinship, ultimately reminding me that within change's embrace, I had discovered a harbor of profound significance.

Having grown up in a city of lesser magnitude, Los Angeles, the City of Angels, drew me in with an undeniable allure. It operated at an accelerated pace, resounding with the echoes of police sirens, helicopters, and the perpetual display of fireworks. However, as an immigrant, I encountered numerous challenges, as is the fate of many who tread this path. Throughout it all, I gleaned invaluable lessons that life bestows upon those who stumble and rise again. I learned the significance of unwavering faith, boundless optimism, and the indomitable spirit to persevere, even when life seemed intent on testing me.

Starting anew felt akin to building an existence from scratch. I was compelled to reset my life's foundations, forge new bonds with friends and kin, make arduous decisions independently, and navigate the complicated bureaucracy to procure necessary documents, for the ones I carried from my homeland had been rendered obsolete, save for my passport, because of their foreign origins.

With meager possessions contained within a single suitcase, housing a scant assortment of clothes and two pairs of shoes. The paltry sum of two hundred dollars offered little solace, leaving me uncertain of how I would survive. Yet, determined to reshape my destiny and fortified by unwavering faith in a higher power, I believed that divine providence had guided me thus far and would continue to pave a path forward. This conviction helped me rise above any circumstance, no matter how seemingly insurmountable, and to summon every ounce of strength to confront the closed doors that lay ahead.

Soccer

Through Ivan's invaluable connections, I managed to secure employment, and my love for soccer led me to discover a nearby soccer group. I began by playing casual pickup games until the day I was introduced to more serious teams. Before long, I found myself attempting soccer tryouts with renowned teams such as the LA Galaxy II. During a pickup soccer game, a friend of mine shared his exciting experience of watching the LA Galaxy team play against their rivals, LA FC, at the Herbalife Nutrition Stadium, the home of LA Galaxy. Intrigued by his story, I decided to research how I could attend a game someday. To my astonishment, while browsing the website, I stumbled upon an advertisement for the LA Galaxy II soccer tryouts. Recognizing this as a golden opportunity for my soccer career, I made a spontaneous decision to sign up for the tryouts instead of merely attending a game as originally intended. Despite facing disappointment at the tryouts, destiny had a different path in store for me. The connections I established with coaches during those endeavors proved to be valuable, as they opened doors to alternative avenues for my soccer journey. Recognizing my potential, some coaches went beyond the confines of the LA Galaxy II, connecting me to other teams that saw my talent and potential. As a result, I found myself embarking on a new chapter filled with exciting opportunities and possibilities beyond my initial expectations.

COVID-19

Yet, the exhilaration proved fleeting. Mere months into my immigrant journey, my resilience was put to the ultimate test as a menacing global pandemic descended upon the world (COVID-19). The pandemic shattered my cherished dreams of pursuing soccer in the city of

Los Angeles, dreams that had bloomed from the very moment I joined a promising soccer team.

Everything came to an abrupt halt. The thought of returning home crossed my mind, but I found myself trapped within the confines of a bustling city gripped by lockdown measures. The pandemic's restrictions cast a surreal pall over the once-familiar streets, leaving me isolated and disconnected from even the few friends who had offered solace and a sense of belonging. Unable to venture beyond my residence, I wrestled with regret, questioning my decision to uproot myself and pursue a new life in a foreign land. Alone within the confines of my home, devoid of human interaction, I confronted a profound sense of desolation.

Police!

It was during one such desolate evening, when I ventured out to purchase groceries only to find the store closed, that a peculiar series of events unfolded.

Drawn by distant fireworks illuminating the darkened sky, I embarked on a solitary journey toward the vibrant spectacle, yet my progress was abruptly halted by the blinding glare of police lights as they converged upon me. A mixture of fear and confusion engulfed me as I complied with their command to stop and raise my hands while desperately seeking an understanding of the unfolding situation. Handcuffed and subjected to a thorough search, I found myself trembling in a state of unparalleled fright. I had never before experienced such terror, the echoes of seeing police shootings online amplifying my apprehension. In this harrowing moment, I fervently whispered prayers, my mind consumed by a torrent of adrenaline that left me unable to focus on anything but the overwhelming sense of panic.

Unaccustomed to encounters with law enforcement, the unfamiliarity intensified my distress. As I attempted to communicate, my initial replies instinctively flowed in my mother tongue, only realizing the necessity of English after a momentary lapse. Upon discerning my accent, one of the police officers adopted a gentler tone and reassured me that everything would be all right. He proceeded to confer with his colleagues, eventually inquiring about my origins and the reason for my presence on that particular street. After clarifying the situation, he cautioned me about the area's reputation and, with a final act of compassion, released me from my restraints.

Relieved of the handcuffs, I made my way home, consumed by an unprecedented sense of despair. The City of Light that had once filled me with boundless excitement and called itself my new home had transformed into a haunting nightmare. Every aspect of the outside world now instilled fear within me, stifling my every step.

I found myself missing home most of the time because it's the place where I feel truly understood. Yet, I felt I had no choice but to remain steadfast and fight because I didn't come all this way just to give up and return home. I refused to accept failure. I had prayed for this opportunity since I was a child, so I continued to push forward. Through it all, I gleaned the invaluable lesson that life bestows upon those who stumble and rise again—that of unwavering faith, boundless optimism, and the indomitable spirit to persevere, even when life seemed intent on testing me.

Treated Like an Immigrant

Little did I fathom the profound impact that the immigrant experience would have on my life. Being an immigrant, I became hyperaware of my accent when I interacted with people who struggled to understand me and constantly pointed out my foreign inflection, inquiring about its origin. It's an ironic realization that one doesn't perceive their own accent because it feels familiar, but to others, it sets us apart and demands explanations with every new encounter. This constant need for understanding sometimes makes me feel like an outsider, as if I don't quite fit in.

I believe in treating others the way I want to be treated, which often leads me to trust people easily. Unfortunately, when I ventured beyond my home country, I extended that trust to others who saw my unfamiliarity with the system and took advantage of it. Some individuals I considered friends exploited my naivety, using me for labor at unfairly low wages or even for free. However, amid this difficult time, God was good to me, revealing who my true friends were and teaching me to trust no one but him.

The life of an immigrant was marked by stark cultural differences. For instance, although it had been helpful in my encounter with the police, the fear of being labeled as mean, bad, or uncaring due to these disparities sometimes makes me hesitant to speak my mind. What may have been acceptable back home is often frowned upon in my current surroundings. I tried to make friends, seeking those who embrace diversity, but their conversations were often alien to me, leaving me silent during social gatherings. Furthermore, when I pursued job opportunities, my accent sometimes led interviewers to doubt my knowledge and qualifications.

As a result, I often ended up taking jobs I didn't enjoy but needed for survival, settling for less by working with a moving company on the weekends, getting a part-time homecare job, and repairing laptops and phones. Despite my education, my credentials from a third-world or less-developed country were often disregarded, hindering my ability to lead a life on par with others. My social standing was new, and my credit score was low or nonexistent, making it difficult to gain trust and make significant purchases.

Transitioning from a tropical climate to one with extreme heat and freezing cold was challenging, but I had to adapt to survive. I also encountered people who didn't appreciate my presence in the country, leaving me yearning to explain my reasons for being here but seldom given the chance. Instead, I was told to go back where I came from, further reinforcing the feeling of being an outsider.

Building a sense of community was arduous as well. In my home country, friendships are often formed spontaneously on the streets, but here, nobody knew anything about me, creating a gap between myself and potential friends. However, even in these circumstances, God brought good friends who become family—those who loved and accepted me for who I am and made an effort to understand my experiences.

Throughout my life, prior to traveling, I naively believed that adapting to a new country or culture would be easy. I couldn't have been more wrong. The hardest part of being a new immigrant is finding people who embrace you as part of their family rather than viewing you as a benefit for their own gain. Being far away from my homeland, especially during significant occasions, is incredibly difficult. Seeing my friends celebrate and enjoy time with their families intensifies my longing for mine. However, they are far away, and I'm left admiring the bonds of other families. Becoming an immigrant didn't solve all my problems as I once thought. Instead, it marked the beginning of a life filled with new problems, cultural differences, and unique solutions that differed from those I knew in my homeland.

Life as an immigrant is a roller coaster ride with its fair share of ups and downs. It's the most significant trial I've ever faced. If I had known what it entailed before becoming an immigrant, it's not something I would have wished for. However, every trial teaches us something, and this is what I've learned so far: no matter where you go, life won't always be smooth sailing. It may start well or not well enough, but I hold on to my faith.

A New Community

Drained by the bustling urban struggles of Los Angeles, I turned to my close friends, a couple with whom I shared a profound bond. I confided in them about my life in LA, laying bare the trials that had woven themselves into the fabric of my existence. After I recounted the relentless battles I faced each day, to my astonishment, they extended an unexpected invitation: "Why not come to Sacramento? You could live with us and, perhaps, forge a new path." Without a second thought, fueled by their genuine care and the chance of a fresh start, I decided to make the daring leap and leave behind the familiar cityscape of LA.

Transitioning from the hustle and bustle of Los Angeles to the more tranquil surroundings of Sacramento up north, I was greeted by an immediate sense of belonging that wrapped around me like a comforting embrace. In this new community, I stumbled upon a haven I had never expected. My introduction to this transformative period came through joining a vibrant youth group that would unknowingly become a cornerstone of my new life.

Little did I know this decision would set me on a path of remarkable personal growth and connection.

In the heart of this welcoming community, I discovered something truly extraordinary. It wasn't just about making friends; it was about forming lasting connections that felt like family ties. Among the many relationships I cultivated, some of the most profound were those with individuals older and wiser than me. The genuine warmth and wisdom they extended to me was profoundly heartening. These extraordinary souls willingly stepped into the roles of mentors and even godparents, offering their guidance as I navigated life's twists and turns. Their presence proved indispensable as I embarked on the intricate journey of maturing both physically and spiritually. As I navigated my newfound surroundings, their collective encouragement ignited an unforeseen spark within me. It was during this time that the seeds of the idea for this book were sown. One of my mentors gently nudged me to consider the impact my life story could have on others. "Derrick, have you ever considered writing a book about your journey? I truly believe that your story holds the power to make a real impact and transform someone's life."

It was this collective encouragement, this rich collection of relationships and newfound belonging, which propelled me to take my story beyond whispered conversations and set it down in writing. The positivity and support of this incredible community, along with the remarkable experiences I had accumulated along the way, would serve as the driving force behind the birth of this very book.

If someone had told me five years ago that I would be an immigrant in the United States, I wouldn't have believed it. At the time, I had closer connections in the United Kingdom, which I thought would be my eventual destination. Yet, God had different plans for me. Now, I walk this path called the American Dream. It's not the familiar road I'm accustomed to, but since it was God's will for me to be in the States, I place my trust in him. I've faced mountains before, and he has been with me through it all. Therefore, I stand firm in him as an immigrant in the land of opportunities, using everything I have to be his hands and feet, whether in big or small ways. I firmly believe that my presence here is in accordance with the will of the Lord, who is good and whose love endures forever. Great are his promises, and I look forward to writing more about what he has already done and what he has in store for me.

About the Author

Derrick Kitayiga, a student at Sierra College, finds fascination and purpose in the intertwining fields of technology and storytelling. Working as a student assistant with the California Department of Public Health (CDPH), he uses his computer science skills to make a meaningful impact. A lover of the written word, he employs storytelling not just to communicate, but to connect, conveying his experiences, passions, and insights through his writings.

Derrick's unwavering faith is the bedrock upon which he builds his life, guiding his journey and infusing a deep sense of purpose in all he does. He has an enduring passion for soccer, considering it much more than a game, but rather a life lesson in teamwork, resilience, and the pursuit of excellence. Derrick's creativity is his constant companion, and with it he explores the intricate complexities that make life truly remarkable.

Online Presence:

Email: Kitayigaderrick9@icloud.com

Instagram: DerrickUganda

Facebook: Kitayiga Derrick M.

www.ingramcontent.com/pod-product-compliance
Lightning Source LLC
Chambersburg PA
CBHW020243130626
46549CB00005B/2033